I Don't Believe In Fairytales

Breaking Anti-Marriage Strongholds

Angeline L. Williams

I Don't Believe in Fairytales
Breaking Anti-Marriage Strongholds
Copyright © 2019 by Angeline L. Williams

ISBN-13: 978-1-7325258-0-1

Published by Redemption Books
www.redemptbooks.com
Our mission is to publish and distribute inspirational products to let the world know that we serve a tangible God who loves and cares about His children.

Book Design by Williams DocuPrep
www.williamsdocuprep.com

Unless otherwise indicated, Scripture quotations are from the: New King James Version of the Bible. Copyright © 1982 by Thomas Nelson. Used by permission. All rights reserved. ESV® Bible (The Holy Bible, English Standard Version®), copyright © 2001 by Crossway, a publishing ministry of Good News Publishers. Used by permission. All rights reserved.

All rights reserved. No part of this publication may be reproduced or transmitted for commercial purposes, except for brief quotations in printed reviews, without the written permission of the author Angeline L. Williams.

Disclaimer and/or Legal Notices: The author and publisher of this book have used their best efforts in preparing this book. This book is for informational purposes only. While every attempt has been made to verify the information provided in this book, the author and publisher make no representation or warranties with respect to accuracy, applicability, fitness, or completeness of the contents. If you wish to apply the ideas contained in this book, you are taking full responsibility for your actions. The author and publisher disclaim any warranties (express or implied), merchantability, or fitness for any particular purpose. The author and publisher shall in no event be held liable to any party for any direct, indirect punitive, special, incidental or other consequential damages arising directly or indirectly from any use of this material, which is provided "as is", and without warranties.

Table of Contents

Preface 2
Once Upon A Time 5
Something in The Milk Ain't Clean? 9
Marriage Is No Fairytale 18
God's Purpose for Marriage 28
God Recognizes Headship 35
We Are at War 42
Satan's Attack on Marriage 48
Sexual Immorality 54
The Spirit of Sabotage 73
Spiritual Strongholds 79
Getting Free 107
Standing in The Gap 119
Soulish Prayers 126
Warfare Scriptures 131
In the Fullness 135
of Time 135
About the Author 141
Meet Jesus 143
Other Books by Angeline 144

Preface

"When the righteous cry for help, the Lord hears and delivers them out of all their troubles." —Psalm 34:17 ESV

Writing this book was challenging because, to correctly share my story and what God told me to share, I had to be transparent and share intimate and personal feelings. It was also tough because I was writing the book while walking through a very painful part of my life. Being vulnerable and sharing your testimony, despite not having it all together, is scary because people can be very harsh and judgmental. especially women against women, even though most have gone through or will go through something similar.

Writing this book was uncomfortable, but it was also empowering. It helped me receive the healing and deliverance that I needed, and that is more important than what anyone thinks of me. I wanted to wait for a romantic ending before publishing, but then I realized that wasn't the message God wanted me to share, and I felt compelled to get the message out.

This is not a book on Christian dating. In this book, you will learn how to recognize the tactics Satan uses to destroy the institution of marriage before couples get to the altar, as well as how to break free of strongholds that prevent you from having a godly marriage. So, if you are looking for dating tips, this book is not for you. If you want to know how to spiritually prepare for marriage, how to recognize and overcome an anti-marriage mindset you may not even realize you have, like I did, or if you are married and having marital issues and need help, the Holy Spirit taught me will be helpful. I pray that you take the time to read and study this message with the Holy Spirit.

I touch on some very touchy topics that may step on some toes, but let me say that nothing in this book is meant as a judgment against anyone. God wants us all to be free to move in the things of God, experience all He has for us, and do what He has called us to do. There are just some things that stand in the way of that, which God wants to deliver us from.

Let us pray:

Our Father, Who art in heaven, hallowed be Thy name; Thy kingdom come; Thy will be done on earth as it is in heaven. Thank You Father, for what You have given me in this book. I come before Your throne, asking You to bless the reader as they study this message. Let their understanding be enlightened. Reveal to them everything You want them to see and understand.

Father, we ask for breakthrough in our lives and in the lives of our future mates. Expose everything that is keeping us from what You promised in Your Word and out of the mouths of the prophets. Show us everything we need to release and repent of. Break every demonic opposition, stronghold, and mindset in our lives and in the lives of our mates. Remove every blockage preventing us from walking in Your promises, and give us the wisdom to stand in Your promises. Let freedom reign, let freedom reign; let freedom reign. In Jesus' name, we pray. Amen.

Angeline L. Williams

Once Upon A Time

"Therefore, my beloved brothers, be steadfast, immovable, always abounding in the work of the Lord, knowing that in the Lord your labor is not in vain." — 1 Corinthians 15:58 ESV

It all started when I reconnected with a man from my past, whom I will refer to as George for the sake of this writing. We went to junior high and senior high school together. I always considered him to be a handsome young man, but there was no romantic interest. We were never anything more than passing acquaintances.

It had been more than 40 years since we'd seen each other. At first, it was just reminiscing, talking about the old neighborhood, and catching up. He asked what street I lived on. When I told him, he asked which house I lived in. I told him, and he said, "Wait a minute, that was Van's house."

"Yep, that's my brother," I said.

"Hold on, so you are the one with the big hips and the big forehead?" I laughed and said, "Yep, that's me."

"Wait a minute! I remember you now. Girl, I had a crush on you, but you never paid me any attention. I used to walk by your house just to look at you. I was crazy about you," he said.

I was surprised when he said that, but I didn't believe him. Then he said that he and my brother used to fight a lot until he got the motorcycle, and he taught him how to ride it. After he said all of that, I believed him, and I was extremely flattered.

As time went on, we talked and got to know each other, and things escalated into a courtship. It was like a fairytale-whirlwind romance. We stayed on the phone, talking for hours like teenagers. It seemed as if love was blooming. George was sweeping me off my feet, and I loved it, but it was time to pray.

After my divorce from my first husband, I asked God to shield me from any man who meant me no good. I didn't want to risk falling in love or getting involved with someone who wasn't marriage material. Or falling for someone God does not want me to be with. Over the years, I'd met a couple of guys to whom I was attracted, and in the very beginning, I prayed, "Father, if this isn't my husband, I don't want to waste my time and get my emotions all worked up.

If he is not the one for me, please put a stop to this relationship now. Don't let this go any further." Each time, something would happen. I would lose interest, or he would lose interest, but things would shut down, sometimes immediately. I was cool with that, and there were no hard feelings between either of us.

I have asked God for specific things in my husband, and it seemed that George exhibited every trait I asked God for in a husband. He prayed with me and was even a little tough, yet humble, like I asked for. He said that maybe God had allowed us to sow our royal oats and brought us together after more than forty years. I was beginning to believe my years of praying for a mate had finally ended.

After a while, we began to talk about marriage and building a future together. He lived in Florida, and I lived in Atlanta. I had wanted to move back to Florida since my daughter went home to be with the Lord in December 2013, so I was jumping at the chance to get back there. However, George felt that it would be best if he moved to Atlanta, and I said okay.

Everything was beautiful. We became engaged and set the wedding date. It looked like the fairytale was on schedule.

Angeline L. Williams

Something in The Milk Ain't Clean?

It was a Saturday morning, and I was so excited to call my friend to tell her about the engagement and invite her to the wedding. It shocked me when she said, "I'm not coming to your wedding, honey! You're not about to marry him!"

"What!" I said. When I asked why, she said, "I just don't feel this marriage is supposed to happen." When I asked why, she said, "I can't put my finger on it, but I have a bad feeling." I told her how wonderful things were with us, how happy he made me, and how well he treated me, but she didn't care about that. She actually mocked me. I told her that I had prayed about us coming together and I had peace, so I was going to go through with it. Then she asked, "Has he been married before?" I said, "Yes, but so have I and so have you." She said, "Well, maybe that's it then."

I Don't Believe in Fairytales

The next day, another person heard me mention that I was engaged. They went to some people and said they had a bad feeling about the engagement, and that they all needed to pray for me. I learned about the prayer request a week later. I asked, "Why didn't anyone come to me with their concerns, and what in the world did y'all pray?"

I don't know what they prayed, and I don't believe either of my friends had any ill feelings towards me or wished me any harm, but I found the timing of everything ironic. The next day, George ended the engagement and our relationship. He said I wasn't over my ex's abuse, and we ended the conversation, which I later realized was an excuse and him casting blame. Just like that, everything was over just as quickly as it had started.

My head was whirling, and I was in shock. I grieved as if someone I loved had died. My vision of getting married was dying. I felt as if I was smack dab in the midst of a demonic attack. I had so many questions, but George wasn't talking, so I could only speculate why he would do such a thing. I spent the next few days trying to make sense out of what had happened. A barrage of emotion was going through me.

Maybe things were moving too fast for him, but he was the one that primarily moved them along, so that didn't make sense. Was he afraid of failing at another marriage? Was he still married? Maybe it was me who was afraid of entering another bad marriage, and I was exhibiting this fear in my actions. Maybe God had indeed shut things down, but why did He wait so long to do it? Why was it necessary for me to hurt so badly? Whatever it was that caused this rift didn't make sense to me, and it felt like a diabolical demonic attack.

"God, did You shut things down? Did You give me warning signs that I ignored? After all these years, why would You allow him to come back into my life only to hurt me? Have I not gotten over what JD did to me, like he said? Did I allow how he treated me to affect how I handled George?"

My ex-husband was a horrible husband, but I forgave him long ago. I have no emotional connection to him. He has passed away, and when I found out that he had died, I did not grieve for him. I even take the blame for what I endured in the marriage because I went against God's wisdom in marrying him.

I paid dearly for that decision, too. The entire marriage, from the week we got married until the day he walked out nine years later, was hell. The marriage was so horrible that I was relieved when he walked out, and I did not miss him. This is why I prayed so hard about my relationship with George. I did not want to be hurt again, and I did not want to go against God's will again.

Even though my first marriage didn't turn out to be what I'd hoped, I loved being married. I believed God had healed me from the trauma of my first marriage, and I was looking forward to being George's wife. I was ready to take what God taught me in my first marriage, couple it with what God would continue to teach me, and be a good wife to George.

Prior to all of this, people were telling me that they had never seen me so happy. It had been 11 years since my divorce. During those years, several close family members passed away, including my mother, my niece, who was like a daughter to me, and my daughter. I had a heart attack and breast cancer, and I went through all of this alone. God and my church family were there, but I can't deny that it felt good to think about having a husband to walk through the next phase of life with and to share life's pains and joys.

After getting over my "how dare you, who are you to judge me? You are the one who has issues with what your ex's did to you attitude," I began to seek God about what had happened and why. It took a few days, but I was finally able to let go of the anger and place our relationship in God's hands to do with what He will. As I prayed, I clearly heard the words, "An enemy has done this; pray."

"Okay, Father, so the enemy came in and blocked the marriage, but why did You allow this? Please help me understand all of this. What am I supposed to get out of this? Am I supposed to stand and fight? Am I supposed to let it go? What do You want me to do?" I didn't want to go against anything that God was doing. I wanted to be free from whatever was blocking me from being married, and I wanted George to be free as well. So, I fasted, prayed, listened, and studied.

I Don't Believe in Fairytales

I was still very emotional, and the enemy kept trying to get me to curse George. Knowing that Satan uses our words to wreak havoc in our lives and in the lives of others, I went into my arsenal—the Word of God. Every time the thought came to say something out of anger regarding George, I prayed God's word over him and asked God to bless him. One passage of scripture I continually prayed was from Ephesians, which are powerful prayers to pray over yourself and others. I include them here, so you can pray them for yourself and others as well:

> *Father, in the name of Jesus, I pray for my friend. I give thanks for the blessing that he is. I pray that You will give him the spirit of wisdom and revelation in knowing who You are, that the eyes of his understanding would be opened to know what is the hope of his calling, the riches of our inheritance in You, and the exceeding greatness of Your power toward us. — taken from Ephesians 1:17-21.*

> *Father, in the name of Jesus, I pray that my friend be strengthened with might in the inner man, that Christ may dwell in his heart through faith; that he, being rooted and grounded in love, may be able to comprehend the*

width, and length, and depth, and height of Christ's love that surpasses knowledge, that he may be filled with all the fullness of God. — taken from Ephesians 3:15-19.

Usually, when relationships end, people are quick to say that it is God's will. That it just wasn't meant to be, that God blocked it. Rarely do people believe the enemy came in to stop what God was doing. Yes, God intervenes to prevent us from getting in situations that will harm us. He's done it for me many times, and if He indeed intervened, then He had good reason and I am okay with His decision. However, this time, after seeking God, said an enemy has done this, pray.

As a believer, there will come a time when you will have to stand on what God said, even when all signs point away from what God is telling you. That may mean drowning out the voices of friends and family, laying down everyone's opinions, and zooming in on what Jesus is saying to you. This is what I felt I had to do. God said to pray, but He didn't say He would bring us back together, so I knew I would have to accept whatever God wanted to do.

I felt that George's decision had nothing to do with me not being over my ex. I felt he was hiding something, which was okay because I realized that God was using the situation to bring healing and deliverance. I knew I needed to use this time to let God work on me. I had some repenting to do, some strongholds to let go of, and I wanted to make sure that I had not made George an idol. Idolatry is a sin that we are repeatedly warned about in the Bible. An idol can be anything you desire more than God.

As a believer, there will come a time when you will have to stand on what God said, even when all signs point away from what God is telling you.

After some soul-searching, I realized that wasn't the case. George and I had talked about me speaking and preaching. He said he wasn't a preacher, but he had no problem supporting and praying for me, helping with the sound, or using his gifts in the church.

Over several days, God began to reveal some things about me and about George that He wanted me to pray about and release. I heard words like "strongholds," "soul ties," "anti-marriage," "marriage breaking," and "fear." So, this is where I focused my prayer and study.

I Don't Believe in Fairytales

Marriage Is No Fairytale

> "Then the Lord God said, "It is not good that the man should be alone; I will make him a helper fit for him." — Genesis 2:18 ESV

There were several reasons why my first marriage failed, all of which were fleshly or carnal. I had made the idea of marriage an idol. I was saved and struggling with the call to preach, and I believed that marriage was necessary for me to fulfill this calling. I didn't think a single woman could pastor a church. I later learned from his best friend that he married me because I was saved, hoping I could rescue him from his drug addiction.

This explained a lot because he never really acted like a married man. The crazy thing is, once I discovered his addiction, I believed that if I prayed fervently enough, God would deliver him. I ignored God's wisdom, and I paid for it. I don't mean God punished me, but living the life of a drug addict's wife was horrible.

Almost immediately after we got married, things began to happen in the marriage that pulled me away from the things of God. Deception was at work. We both lost sight of the Savior, Jesus Christ. In that marriage, I learned a valuable lesson: Let God lead you in everything, especially something as serious as marriage.

I learned that I can't change anyone who doesn't want to change, or do the work to change. People have to decide to change on their own, that's the point of free will. I also learned not to let anything, or anyone draw you away from God. I can't even put into words the emptiness I felt. For years, I felt like I was hiding from God because I knew that I had gone against His will and married despite the gigantic red flags.

Even after a failed marriage, I still want to experience a godly marriage. I understood that my priority had to be God this time, which wasn't a problem because I missed the intimate relationship I had with my Father during that marriage. I used the time after my divorce to draw closer to God and let Him heal me.

Many Christian men and women, young and old, have been praying for a life companion for some time, going from relationship to relationship, hoping the next one will be "the one." There could be many reasons why the answer is delayed. Keep in mind that God loves both of you. He may still be preparing both of you before He brings you two together. Just because it is taking some time doesn't mean that God is not answering the prayer. One or the other may not even know why God created marriage, let alone be prepared for it. One or the other may be asking amiss. One or the other may be dealing with some unconfessed sin, demonic oppression, ungodly strongholds, or soul ties that need to be dealt with.

Marriage is, first of all, a God thing! It is a part of our divine inheritance from God. Marriage was the first institution that the Lord instituted or created, right there in the

Garden of Eden. He is the One who started it, and He defends it very passionately. When He instituted marriage, God had a divine purpose and a plan for it. Marriage is a picture of God's great love for us (Ephesians 5:28–33). Through marriage between a man and a woman, God fulfills His destiny for them while advancing His kingdom. Even if you have been married before and it did not work, God still has a purpose and a plan for it.

Many people have a fairytale image of marriage. Little girls dream of their wedding ceremony and see themselves surrounded by friends and loved ones, wearing a beautiful gown, standing with a handsome groom ready to sweep them off their feet, and the two riding off into the sunset, living happily ever after. I believe that with God all things are possible, so yes, I believe happily ever after is possible, but marriage is no fairytale; it is serious business.

While Satan plays a huge part, relationships and engagements end, and divorces occur because of the way some people view marriage. Some have a casual, take-it-or-leave-it attitude toward marriage. Many people enter marriage with a self-centered point of view; they view it as a way of finding love, happiness, and companionship.

They marry for physical attraction or sex. These are important components of marriage, but they are not good reasons to marry. And some marry for the idea of being married. God's design for marriage between a man and a woman is not about them at all; it is about God. Marriage is a sacred institution, holy before God, and it has great significance in the spiritual realm. God never intended for His creation to be single, for He said, "It is not good that the man should be alone; I will make a helpmeet for him" (Genesis 2:18).

The first Father to give away His daughter to her husband was God, instituting a new kind of relationship called marriage.

Does this mean a marriage cannot be successful without God at the helm? No, it does not, but Christian marriages are to reflect God's image: Then God said, *"Let us make man in our image, in our likeness, and let them rule over the fish of the sea and the birds of the air, over the livestock, over all the earth, and over all the creatures that move along the ground. So, God created man in his own image, in the image of God he created him; male and female he created them."* — Genesis 1:26-27

From the beginning, God had a plan for the family— a husband and wife coming together body, soul, and spirit, and out of their union comes forth new life — children. Churches, cities, and nations all stand on the strength of the family. When the family began to break down, so did everything else.

Again, it all started at creation, when the all-knowing God created man, He created him male and female, knowing that man would need a companion (Genesis 1:27). It is at the creation of male and female that we see God's design for marriage and family.

When God created the perfect companion for Adam, He didn't create her from the dust like He did Adam. He didn't speak her into existence like He did the firmament, the waters, or the trees and vegetation. No, He put Adam to sleep, and then He took one of his ribs and created a perfect companion for Adam.

Like Adam, Eve was a perfect creation, patterned after

God's image and likeness. Everything about her was unique, yet she was not created as a separate being; she was made from a part of Adam. Like Adam, Eve was a perfect creation patterned after God's image and likeness (Genesis 1:27). She was a helper fit for him—a counterpart, his complement, created to strengthen him. She was a wife. Then God brought Eve to Adam.

Adam looked at her and saw what a beautiful creation she was, and he exclaimed, "This is now bone of my bones and flesh of my flesh; she shall be called Woman, because she was taken out of Man!" Then God decreed, *"Therefore shall a man leave his father and his mother and shall cleave unto his wife: and they shall be one flesh"* (Genesis 1:2).

The Hebrew word for "cleave" is *"dabaq"* which means 'to cling or stick to', to adhere to as if with glue, to be glued. So, one could say that when a man and woman marry, they become "glued" to each other.

It is God who ordains and performs the uniting of flesh. The first time He did so was in The Garden. When He took a rib from Adam's side and created Eve they were in fact "one flesh." Adam recognized Eve a was part of him because he said, "This at last is bone of my bones and flesh of my flesh; she shall be called Woman, because she was taken out of Man."

The words "cleave unto his wife" and "they shall be one flesh" indicate that God intends marriage to be a sacred, lifelong covenant filled with self-sacrifice, love, and honor.

Marriage is a covenant, a holy agreement between God and His children. It is not a contract or agreement that one can walk away from whenever one wants. Tragically, this is what is common today among people both inside and outside of the church.

In Malachi 2:13 God also speaks of marriage as a covenant:

"This is another thing you do: you cover the altar of the Lord with tears, with weeping and with groaning, because He no longer regards the offering or accepts it with favor from your hand. Yet you say, 'For what reason?' Because the Lord has been a witness between you and the

wife of your youth, against whom you have dealt treacherously, though she is your companion and your wife by covenant." — *Malachi 2:13*

This scripture says that marriage is a covenant, witnessed, and sealed by God. In regard to marriage, a covenant is a holy promise to God between a man and a woman to care for, love, and be faithful to each other for life and to carry out God's plan in their lives.

In biblical days covenants were binding and can only be broken when one party dies, even if new circumstances like sickness and changes in finances occur. The high divorce rates of today indicate that too many people see marriage as just an agreement that can be broken at will, rather than a spiritual covenant.

"And God blessed them, and God said unto them, be fruitful, and multiply, and replenish the earth, and subdue it: and have dominion over the fish of the sea, and over the fowl of the air, and over every living thing that moveth upon the earth." — *Genesis 1:28 (KJV)*

Then, after God performed the first joining of flesh at

creation, moving forward, a man and a woman become one flesh through sex. Scripture says God created sex for a man and woman in a marriage relationship.

> *"Marriage is honourable in all, and the bed undefiled: but whoremongers and adulterers God will judge." — Hebrews 13:4 (KJV)*

> *"(1) Now about those questions you asked in your last letter: my answer is that if you do not marry, it is good. 2 But usually it is best to be married, each man having his own wife, and each woman having her own husband, because otherwise you might fall back into sin." — 1 Corinthians 7:1–2 (KJV)*

I Don't Believe in Fairytales

God's Purpose for Marriage

"So they are no longer two, but one flesh. What therefore God has joined together, let no man separate." —Matthew 19:6

Marriage is a death to the "me-myself and I" mentality and a birth to a mutual identity in each other. One flesh. Many people don't realize it and may not even agree, but God's picture of marriage is what every couple wants deep down inside. Christians especially desire to have an Ephesians Five marriage.

In Ephesians 5:21-33 God gives us a picture of a perfect marriage, with the wife submitting to the husband as to the Lord and the husband loving his wife like Christ loves the church. Ladies according to the Word we are to submit to our husband in the same manner as we submit to Jesus.

> *"Therefore, just as the church is subject to Christ, so let the wives be to their own husbands in everything."*— Ephesians 5:24

Many women have issues with this command because they think this mindset is outdated, and that it means that women are inferior to men, but that is simply not true. Although God ordained that the man be the head of the family, in His sight men and women are spiritual equals. Galatians 3:28 says:

> *"There is neither Jew nor Greek, there is neither slave nor free man, there is neither male nor female; for you are all one in Christ Jesus."*

So, you see, God doesn't see women as inferior, inadequate, or less important, than men. Both the husband and the wife have equal standing and equal spiritual privileges in Christ because we are all united with Him in the same way. We have different roles, different assignments, and different functions, but we are equal in God.

Yes, the husband is the head of the home, but he is not to be a dictator, neither is he to demean his wife or to treat her as a slave. In fact, the Bible says that the way a man treats his wife interferes with his prayer life.

> "Likewise, husbands, live with your wives in an understanding way, showing honor to the woman as the weaker vessel, since they are heirs with you of the grace of life, so that your prayers may not be hindered. — 1 Peter 3:7 (ESV)

Men are responsible for how they show love to their wife, no matter how she responds to them. Men who mistreat and abuse their wives turn God into their enemy. This is not a good place to be. God does not hold you responsible for what your wife does and says to you, but He will hold you responsible for how you love her.

> (28) So husbands ought to love their own wives as their own bodies; he who loves his wife loves himself. (29) For no one ever hated his own flesh, but nourishes and cherishes it, just as the Lord does the church." — Ephesians 5:28-29

Men are bigger and physically stronger than women so, even though there are some women who build up their bodies and try to function in society as a man, the Bible says the woman is the weaker vessel. She can be built like a football player, but she is still the weaker vessel.

> *A help meet is not a barefoot in the kitchen kind of help, it is a God ordained, life-saving, powerful help that comes with tremendous power.*

Men and women are wired differently also. God designed the woman's psyche to be responsive to being handled gently. I know this to be true for me. As tough and strong as some think I am, I don't like to argue, be yelled at or handled roughly. Chivalry may not be popular, but it is not dead, at least not to me.

Yes, please open my doors, pull out my chair, make me feel safe and secure in your strong arms and treat me like the queen that I am, because I am going to treat you like the king that you are. Nope, I am not a women's libber. I haven't burned and don't plan on burning any bras.

God made men to be leaders, decision-makers, and problem solvers. God made woman for man; to be man's help meet. A help meet is compatible physically, emotionally, and spiritually with her husband. She is the nurturer of the home (Genesis 2:18).

Like submission, there are some women who have a problem accepting the fact that we were created to be a man's helpmeet. I believe this is due to a lack of understanding. So, let's look a little closer to gain more understanding.

The Hebrew word for helper is "ezer", which is used several times in the Old Testament in reference to someone who is very strong and capable coming to the rescue of another in serious trouble! Most of the references are about God Himself as He helps, rescues, and delivers mankind!

So being a helper isn't the barefoot and in the kitchen kind of help, it is a life-saving, powerful help that comes with tremendous power. This brings to mind the phrase, "Behind every great man there's a great woman."

It is the wife's responsibility to help the husband become all that God wants him to be, in the same way that God helps us become who He wants us to be. So how can you be a good helpmeet?

> *"(22) Wives, submit to your own husbands, as to the Lord. (23) For the husband is the head of the wife even as Christ is the head of the church, his body, and is himself its Savior. (24) Now as the church submits to Christ, so also wives should submit in everything to their husbands." — Ephesians 5:22-24 (ESV)*

If we follow the example of Christ in His relationship with the Church, we will be the helper God has called us to be. A good wife respects her husband and recognizes that he is called to be the "head" of the family, by responding positively to his leadership, listening to him, and valuing his opinions. She admires his values and character, she is considerate of his needs, and she entrusts her care to him.

I learned in my first marriage that if a husband is not submitted to God, it is difficult for a wife to submit to him as unto the Lord. This will create problems in the home and give the enemy a foothold in the marriage. I also learned just as husbands are responsible for how they treat their wives, we are responsible for how we show love to our husband. Regardless of how they act toward us, whether they respond in love and whether they follow God's way or not. This can be tough, but it is not impossible with the help of the Holy Spirit.

As Christians, the Word of God is our guide in how we handle situations that arise in our life. Remember, we are not responsible for another person's actions, but we are responsible for how we treat others.

While women are called to be helpmeets, we can also perform supporting roles inside and outside of ministry life. The Bible gives us strong examples of women who did great things either ahead of men or alongside of men. For example, Deborah led Barak (Judges 4) and Priscilla served God alongside Aquila, her husband (Acts 18:18-28).

Angeline L. Williams

God Recognizes Headship

Whether you are waiting to be married or are already married, it is important to understand that in God's order of the family unit, the man is the head of the household. God set up man's headship at creation by creating Adam and giving him instructions on how to live before He created Eve.

> "*15 The Lord God took the man and put him in the garden of Eden to work it and keep it. 16 And the Lord God commanded the man, saying, "You may surely eat of every tree of the garden, 17 but of the tree of the knowledge of good and evil you shall not eat, for in the day that you eat of it you shall surely die."*
>
> *18 Then the Lord God said, "It is not good that the man should be alone; I will make him a helper fit for him. 19 Now out of the ground the Lord God had formed every beast of the field and every bird of the heavens and*

brought them to the man to see what he would call them. And whatever the man called every living creature, that was its name. [20] The man gave names to all livestock and to the birds of the heavens and to every beast of the field. But for Adam there was not found a helper fit for him.

[21] So the Lord God caused a deep sleep to fall upon the man, and while he slept took one of his ribs and closed up its place with flesh. [22] And the rib that the Lord God had taken from the man he made into a woman and brought her to the man. [23] Then the man said, "This at last is bone of my bones and flesh of my flesh; she shall be called Woman, because she was taken out of Man." — Genesis 2:15–23

Notice that it was after God set Adam's headship and authority over all creation that He created Eve. He then brought Eve to Adam. The first Father to give away his daughter to her husband was God, instituting a new kind of relationship called marriage. Then He spoke the design for every future marriage:

"Therefore a man shall leave his father and mother and be joined to his wife, and they shall become one flesh." —

Genesis 2:24

Look at that, the man moves out from under his parents' authority and establishes his own headship and authority over his family. The woman moves from under her father to being under her husband. This is God's definition of marriage.

God sees the man as the priest or shepherd of the home, therefore being the head of the family is a big responsibility and should not be taken lightly. It is to the man and through the man that God communicates His word to the family. His assignment is to provide spiritual leadership for everyone in the home, to ensure they can all grow to be all God desires them to be.

In the Bible, bread represents the Word of God. In the Old Testament three times a year the men were required to come before God and keep the Feast of Unleavened Bread, the Feast of Harvest, and the Feast of Ingathering (Exodus 23:13-17). Eating unleavened bread in the Bible symbolizes eating the pure Word of God, untainted by the philosophies and doctrines of man. This is interesting because Paul said that the husband is to sanctify and cleanse his wife by the washing of water with the word (Ephesians 5:26).

"25 Husbands, love your wives, as Christ loved the church

and gave himself up for her, 26 that he might sanctify her, having cleansed her by the washing of water with the word" — Ephesians 5:26

To "sanctify" means to set apart or make holy. Christ sanctifies us at salvation. Husbands are to model their love on the sanctifying relationship of Christ and the church. Cleansing her with the washing of water by the word means the husband has a responsibility as the God ordained leader and priest to help his wife grow spiritually.

God commanding the man to come before Him each year as the priest of the home for the Feast of Unleavened Bread indicates that it was up to the man to keep his house together in the ways of the LORD like a shepherd.

God sees the man as the priest or shepherd of the home. Being the head of the family is a big responsibility and should not be taken lightly.

The husband represents Christ in the home; therefore he must ensure that the wife is well resourced and the children well discipled. So, not only does it mean that it is the man's responsibility to carry the weight of providing for, protecting, and shepherding the family, it also means that husbands hold the key to a flourishing marriage.

The Apostle Paul talked about the headship of the husband:

> "But I want you to know that the head of every man is Christ, the head of woman is man, and the head of Christ is God." —1 Corinthians 11:3

> "For the husband is head of the wife, as also Christ is head of the church; and He is the Savior of the body." — Ephesians 5:23

Christ, the Divine Husband showed the strongest love ever for the Church. He sacrificed Himself for it. He is attentive to its needs, and He bears it like we would do for the parts of our own body. This is how husbands ought to love their wives.

> "[25] Husbands, love your wives, as Christ loved the church and gave himself up for her, [26] that he might sanctify her, having cleansed her by the washing of water with the word, [27] so that he might present the church to himself in splendor, without spot or wrinkle or any such thing, that she might be holy and without blemish. [28] In the same way husbands should love their wives as their own bodies. He

who loves his wife loves himself." — *Ephesians 5:25-28*

God did not assign the roles of husbands and wives based upon ability or what one knows. So, even if his wife is more mature in the Word than the husband, God has still given the leadership role to the husband.

Because God has ordained him as the head of the family, there is no need for the husband to be intimidated by his wife's knowledge and no need for the wife to feel superior to her husband.

As he studies the Word for himself, he should share with his wife what he learns, speak the word over her, and bless her. He should pray for her, and with her. It would help them both if he encourages his wife to share what she knows and to continue her growth. I can't imagine a woman who would not appreciate, respect, trust and submit to a man who does this.

Many men today talk about being the head, or the man of the house, but they don't read their Bible, won't take their family to church, and don't pray to God or spend time with Him. If the man is not receiving instruction from his head (Christ) how can he properly lead his family as set forth by God?

The husband must be willing to lead, protect, and shepherd his family, and the wife must be willing to submit to his leadership in order for the family unit to function as God intends. Conflict will occur in marriage, but if both partners are submitted to Christ, they will be minimal, and between the three of you, resolution will always come. Becoming a competent head or suitable helpmeet is a process that requires prayer, intentional focus, submission, and devotion to God and His plans.

We Are at War

"Be sober, be vigilant; because your adversary the devil walks about like a roaring lion, seeking whom he may devour. Resist him, steadfast in the faith, knowing that the same sufferings are experienced by your brotherhood in the world" (1 Peter 5:8,9).

God is a Spirit, and the devil is also a spirit. God is all that is holy and good. In contrast, Satan, the devil, is all that is evil and wicked. Jesus called Satan the father of lies and all that is false (John 8:44). Everything that takes place in the physical world is connected to the war that is continuously waged in the spiritual world. Satan somehow convinced one-third of heaven's angels to join him in rebellion against God:

"14 You were the anointed cherub who covers; I established you; You were on the holy mountain of God; You walked back and forth in the midst of fiery stones. 15 You were perfect in your ways from the day you were created,

till iniquity was found in you. **16** *"By the abundance of your trading You became filled with violence within, and you sinned; Therefore I cast you as a profane thing out of the mountain of God; And I destroyed you, O covering cherub, From the midst of the fiery stones.* — *Ezekiel 28:14-16 (NKJV)*

So, this great angelic being who was created to worship God got greedy for power and tried to overthrow heaven. War broke out and He was kicked out by Michael, an angel who fought on God's behalf.

*"****7*** *And war broke out in heaven: Michael and his angels fought with the dragon; and the dragon and his angels fought,* ***8*** *but they did not prevail, nor was a place found for them in heaven any longer.* ***9*** *So the great dragon was cast out, that serpent of old, called the Devil and Satan, who deceives the whole world; he was cast to the earth, and his angels were cast out with him."* — *Revelation 12:7-9 (NKJV)*

So now, whether we believe it or not; whether we are aware of it or not, Satan and those angels fight against God and humanity, especially Christians, every day. This war is fought in the spiritual realm. The mind is the battleground.

Unfortunately, most people tend to see their problems and struggles in non-spiritual terms, which makes them seek non-spiritual solutions.

Satan is a created being, so he is not omnipresent, He can only be in one place at a time, so he works through the vast army of demon spirits that were thrown out of heaven with him. When someone says, "The devil has been trying to stop me," it's unlikely that Satan himself is doing it; it is probably one of his demons on assignment.

Most people give Satan too much credit. They blame him for everything from a flat tire to the refrigerator breaking down. Truth is a flat tire could be the result of running over a nail. The refrigerator may just be old. Appliances don't last forever. Every obstacle or setback we face in life is not rooted in demonic activity.

Satan and his demons are not behind every problem, but he appreciates the credit. He wants us to think that he has the power to do these things. He wants us to think his power is greater than God's. He wants us to doubt God's promise that He will care for us no matter the situation or circumstance we find ourselves in.

What we magnify tends to manifest (Job 3:25). So, although we are told to be sober, and vigilant because the devil seeks to devour us (1 Peter 5:8), being hyper-focused on identifying demons and tearing down strongholds can actually perpetuate the vicious cycle. Magnify the devil, and he looks bigger and bigger in your eyes. Magnify the problem rather than the promise, and the problem gets bigger. Magnify Jesus, and His glory inspires you to overcome by His grace.

In Ephesians 6:12, Paul urges us to remember that we do not wrestle against flesh and blood, but against principalities, against powers, against the rulers of the darkness, against spiritual hosts of wickedness in the heavenly places, the spiritual realm. This means that the battle is not against your spouse, your child, your neighbor, or even your own weaknesses; it is spiritual.

Lashing out at those who hurt us may make us feel better for a moment, but in the end, nothing is resolved. It usually only makes matters worse.

This can be a hard truth to accept because when we are wronged, we want someone or something to lash out at. Lashing out at those who hurt you may make you feel better for a moment, but in the end, nothing is resolved, and it usually only makes matters worse. This is how operating in "the flesh" works.

Our flesh, sometimes called the "sin nature," is that rebellious, unruly, and stubborn part of us that does not want to be told what to do. It hates to be under authority or to yield to anything other than its own desires. It is stubborn, it refuses correction, and it does not want to have anything to do with God and His ways. Nothing good comes from living by the flesh. When living according to the way of God seems hard, remember we are not called to live it by ourselves. The Holy Spirit is our helper and teacher. Ask Him for help.

The flesh is always fighting against our spirit, and the spirit is always fighting against our flesh. We will deal with our flesh until we get to heaven. No matter how long we have been saved, we cannot train our flesh to live the Christian life, so we must learn to bring our flesh under subjection to the Word of God. How do you know if you're in the flesh? If you are desiring something forbidden or something that goes against God's word, you are operating in the flesh.

"5 For those who live according to the flesh set their minds on the things of the flesh, but those who live according to

the Spirit, the things of the Spirit. ⁶ *For to be carnally minded is death, but to be spiritually minded is life and peace.* ⁷ *Because the carnal mind is enmity against God; for it is not subject to the law of God, nor indeed can be.* ⁸ *So then, those who are in the flesh cannot please God." — Romans 8:5-8 (NKJV)*

I Don't Believe in Fairytales

Satan's Attack on Marriage

"So then, they are no longer two but one flesh. Therefore what God has joined together, let not man separate." — Matthew 19:6

Like everything else God created, Satan hates marriage, so he tries to undermine and distort the witness of marriage. We can see how the biblical definition of marriage has come under increasing attack in recent years. Nothing shows the devil's influence on today's society quite like the assault on marriage and the family unit. With the high divorce rate to same-sex marriage, we can see Satan is having a field day trying to destroy the family unit.

Satan hates that a husband and wife can cleave to one another in God. He hates the love and honor that takes place between the husband, the wife and God. So, he tries to break up existing relationships to prevent marriages from taking place. He plants fear, casts doubt, misuses

Scripture, and uses other schemes to go after children of God. I believe this is why so many couples have such silly arguments and run with fear just before the wedding. Then, if he can't stop the marriage from happening, he continues to work throughout the marriage to destroy it.

Every marriage has two enemies: selfishness and Satan, and the battle starts before marriage.

As I continued to seek God, He flashed scenes of my life across my mind. I could clearly see some patterns in my life and George's life that needed addressing; some strongholds that we both needed to overcome. For instance, I've been engaged three times and married once, but each relationship ended in the seventh year. It was as if God said, "Okay, that's enough!" George has been married more than once. He said neither of his marriages lasted more than five years. God has done some miraculous things in both of our lives; however, there is still work to be done.

On the surface, some might say that neither of us was a suitable relationship candidate, but they would be basing their thoughts on our past. I know for sure that I am not the same woman I was years ago. Of course, I am still a work in progress, but Christ and God's Word have changed me from the inside out. As I got to know George, I came to believe the same thing about him.

A friend of mine, Deborah, made a statement that confirmed what I believe about judging people based on their past. She said:

> *While the past does sometimes repeat itself, people do change and grow. I know this for sure because I have changed drastically from who I used to be. There are also different accounts of how the past actually went. Someone told me that they were told to be careful of a person they are in a relationship with. People will have different sides of the story.*
>
> *When it comes to instances such as this my advice is to take all things into account. How has the person treated you so far? And what about the person that told you this? What are their motives? Sincere? Maybe, but probably not.*
>
> *When you have seeds of doubt sown into your mind about someone it can actually change how you communicate with them. Causing problems where there were none, and you can treat them unfairly because of their past, when you weren't even there.*

Bringing up someone's past is not fair. Unless you want to communicate about it in a fair way. For what? To ease your mind. Do you want to bring up your own past? Chances are if you treat someone kind and loving they will return the same. Why cause problems in a new relationship over the past? If there are problems with a person, you will see it soon enough. You won't need anyone else to tell you."

Deborah is so on point with what I was hearing in my spirit about relationships. In my experience, you can begin looking at the person sideways, out of the corner of your eye, waiting for them to mess up and make a mistake because of something someone else told you.

Wisdom says in Proverbs 16:28: *"A dishonest man spreads strife, and a whisperer separates close friends."* When someone comes to you gossiping about someone else you don't have to listen. In fact, Wisdom says in Proverbs 20:19 *"do not associate with a simple babbler."*

Have you ever had someone treat you differently after you revealed something about yourself? How did it make you feel? Did you begin to walk around on pins and needles, trying not to make a mistake? Think about it, isn't that a miserable way to live?

Listen, once we are saved and born again, we become new creations in Christ. Our sin slate is wiped clean. We are given a new start in this life. That goes for you, your saved potential mate, and your saved spouse! God never holds our past against us, and we shouldn't hold anyone else's past against them.

Holding someone's past against them can actually make you more hurt. For instance, what if you confront the person and they say, "No, I didn't do that?" Or what if they say, "So what if I did do it? What are you going to do about it?" What are you going to do after that? Hopefully, you will just walk away, but the bottom line is that you are left with even more anger and hurt and no resolution. It's just better to let it go, let the people off the hook, and then let God deal with you and them.

Think about it. Do you want someone constantly bringing up your past and holding it against you? Try treating others the way you want to be treated. Be kind and loving, and more than likely, they will return the same. Why cause problems in a new relationship over the past?

Have you been feeling like a victim? When we were kids, teens, or adults, we all felt emotional pain, but we can't stay there, you must move past the hurt. It may feel good to blame others or to be the victim, but holding onto the past only holds your future hostage. If this is what you've been doing, then you're missing out on your present. It's time to move on. To accept new joy and happiness into your life, you must make space for it. If your heart is filled with pain and hurt, how can you be open to anything new? The past is the past; leave it there.

Openness and honesty are essential components for building a relationship. Everyone deserves to know who they are getting involved with, but I've learned that it is not necessary to reveal every detail about your life and your past, especially in new relationships, nor is it necessary to know everything about your potential mate's past right away. If I had not shared so much about my previous marriage with George, he would not have been able to say, "You haven't gotten over what your ex did to you."

I've learned that God will not let us be ignorant of anything we need to know. So, if there is something about another person that God wants you to know, He will reveal it. He'll set things up so that everything you need to share and learn will take place at the appointed time. So, trust God with you and all that concerns you.

Sexual Immorality

Before I delve into this section, I want to be upfront and admit that before God revealed His truth about sexual immorality, I participated sinned in this area. The journey of sexual immorality for me started when a relative sexually assaulted me when I was eleven years old. This incident caused a lot of problems for me in the future. After that, I left and moved with my mother, where I experienced three more instances of sexual assault. Rape and molestation was prevalent in my environment, and the enemy was using it to destroy lives. The family patriarchs on both sides of my family turned a blind eye to what was going on in the family.

I began to feel as if something was wrong with me—that I was singled out to be abused no matter where I went. I felt so alone and unloved. I began equating sex with love. I was searching for love in all the wrong places, torn between living a life for God and living by my own way and the world. Promiscuity and living in sin all seemed like the natural thing to do in my quest for true love.

As I grew closer to God, I realized how wrong all of this was, and that it was not what God intended for His children. I repented for my actions and ignorance, and God forgave me, healed me, delivered me, and kept me when I allowed Him to. One thing I have realized is that the enemy uses the spirits of rape and molestation to distort a child's understanding of love and family. Sexual violence generates both negative and positive spiritual outcomes for female and male survivors.

Like marriage, God created sex for a purpose: to be enjoyed by one man and one woman within the bonds of marriage as a means of intimacy and procreation, and because He loves us, He made it pleasurable. Sex in any other context is an act of rebellion against God.

Satan uses all kinds of devices to draw us into sin, disbelief, and disobedience to God, and sexual immorality is certainly one of his deadliest tools. Satan has worked hard to normalize it. In society, sexual immorality is glorified; adultery, premarital sex, and homosexuality are common. Just about every television show has a sex scene within the first few minutes, averaging almost six sex scenes per hour.

Reality TV shows, commercials, and the internet all make sexual immorality seem like the normal thing to do.

What is sexual immorality? According to the Bible, sexual immorality is any sexual expression outside of marriage between a man and a woman, which God instituted. It is a sin that entails a wide range of illicit sexual activity. In the Old Testament, God instituted laws that prohibited adultery and other forms of sexual misconduct, such as incest and rape. In the New Testament, Jesus taught that all sexual relationships outside of marriage are sin. This would include fornication, adultery, incest, rape, homosexuality, and other forms of sexual misconduct. He also taught that lust in the heart is just as wrong as sexual sin in the flesh.

"For out of the heart come evil thoughts—murder, adultery, sexual immorality, theft, false testimony, slander".

The Greek word for "sexual immorality" in this verse is porneia, which can also be translated as "fornication". (Matthew 15:19) All of these sexual sins open a spiritual door for the enemy to attack us. Sexual immorality does not honor God. In this chapter, we will examine how they work and how to overcome them so that the enemy can no longer attack us.

What's The Big Deal?

God considers it a grave sin.

- In 1 Corinthians 6:13 it says, *"The body is not meant for sexual immorality, but for the Lord, and the Lord for the body."*

- Ephesians 5:3 says, *"But sexual immorality and all impurity or covetousness must not even be named among you, as is proper among saints."*

- 1 Thessalonians 4:3 says *"For this is the will of God, your sanctification: that you abstain from sexual immorality;"*

Almost every book of the Bible speaks out against sexual immorality, yet its warnings are often dismissed, brushed aside as minor, or irrelevant, or written off as outdated even among Christians. Let's look closely at what Paul says about sexual immorality in 1 Corinthians 6:12-20

> *"[12] I have the right to do anything," you say—but not everything is beneficial. "I have the right to do anything"—but I will not be mastered by anything. [13] You say, "Food for the stomach and the stomach for food, and God will destroy them both." The body, however, is not meant for sexual immorality but for the Lord, and the Lord for the body. [14]*

By his power God raised the Lord from the dead, and he will raise us also. ¹⁵ *Do you not know that your bodies are members of Christ himself? Shall I then take the members of Christ and unite them with a prostitute? Never!* ¹⁶ *Do you not know that he who unites himself with a prostitute is one with her in body? For it is said, "The two will become one flesh."* ¹⁷ *But whoever is united with the Lord is one with him in spirit.*

¹⁸ *Flee from sexual immorality. All other sins a person commits are outside the body, but whoever sins sexually, sins against their own body.* ¹⁹ *Do you not know that your bodies are temples of the Holy Spirit, who is in you, whom you have received from God? You are not your own;* ²⁰ *you were bought at a price. Therefore honor God with your bodies." (1 Corinthians 6:12-20).*

Paul was writing to the Corinthians, who had a casual attitude about sexual immorality. Despite their awareness of the power of Jesus' blood and grace, they chose to dishonor God through various forms of sin and sexual immorality. All sin separates us from God, but sexual sin is unique, which is why we are to "flee from sexual immorality."

Paul explains why sexual immorality is so significant

(using the analogy of a believer engaging in sex with a prostitute). He cautions that sex is more than a mere bodily function; God designed it to be limited within the boundary of a covenant marriage between one man and one woman, to unite a man and a woman into one body in marriage.

If we are in Christ, our bodies are temples, holy places where the Holy Spirit lives. Our bodies belong to God. Engaging in sexual activities outside of marriage drags Christ into that ungodly union with us. We should not treat God's temple so disrespectfully. We should not do as we please with God's temple.

Effects Of Sexual Sin

Sexual immorality is all around us. There is definitely a spirit of deception at work, lulling so many people into complacency about premarital sex. No matter what people are doing today, Christians must remember that engaging in premarital sex dishonors God. Sexual sin, on its own, does not send anyone to hell any more than a person's morality can secure them a place in heaven. Regardless of how moral or immoral a person's outward behavior may be, people go to hell because they have never believed in Jesus' redemptive work on the cross.

Though sexual sin is forgivable in Christ, there are consequences to consider. Sexual sin has spiritual significance and can have serious consequences. When sexual sin operates in your body, it prevents God from using you as He desires. Sexual immorality and the practice of willful sin of any kind will hinder a child of God from growing and operating in the things of God.

People make up all kinds of excuses to justify their sin when they don't want to leave it alone. People make up all kinds of excuses to justify sin, in this case, premarital sex. We are getting married anyway, so what's the harm? What if we get married and we aren't sexually compatible? How will you know if you're sexually compatible? No one buys shoes before trying them on. This is a viewpoint I previously held. This rationality does not take into account God's love for us or what a Christian marriage is all about. God loves us and knows us better than we know ourselves. He knows what makes us happy.

When God created Eve for Adam, He said, "I will make a suitable partner for him" (Genesis 2:18). So if He chooses a mate for us, it stands to reason that you will complement each other in every area. Trust God that you will be sexually compatible with your future spouse. The sex will be enjoyable, as well as honoring God. Many people have various reasons for not adhering to God's word, but it's important to remember that marriage should mirror the love between Christ and His church. Christ doesn't love the church because we do everything the way that He wants to. He loves us even when we don't. A healthy Christian marriage isn't about compatibility, but about God's purpose.

Blatant sexual sin opens spiritual doors with another person, and more often than not, you don't know what lies behind those doors. The world warns people not to have protected sex because of the risk of contracting AIDS or STDs. They warn that having sex with someone means having sex with everyone they've had sex with prior to you. That is a scary thought!

If you know you have had unprotected sex and have not contracted AIDS or an STD, this is a good place to thank and praise God for shielding you from the dangers thus far. This is a warning in the natural realm, but there is more that takes place in the spiritual realm.

So what does this mean? Well, when we engage in sexual sin, it is against our bodies. God designed sexual intercourse as a spiritual bond between a husband and wife. Genesis 2:24 says, "Therefore a man shall leave his father and his mother and hold fast to his wife, and they two shall become one flesh." Whether in marriage or not, joining sexually with another person not only physically unites you as one flesh, but it also forges a spiritual tie.

Listen!! When you do this, you open yourself up spiritually. The point here is that you don't know where the other person has been, what they have been involved with, or what spirits they've united themselves with that are now united with you. In other words, when you lay down with a person, you don't know what you're getting up with.

God is not trying to be cruel by saying we should flee sexual immorality; He is trying to protect us from evil powers, principalities, rulers of the darkness of this age, and spiritual hosts of wickedness in the heavenly places who are looking for a home. This knowledge should compel us to hold to God's warning. Remember, Ecclesiastes 10:8b says, *"whoso breaketh a hedge, a serpent shall bite him.*

Although we have been born again in our inner man (spirit), we still live in our old body (flesh) with its evil desires. Paul called it a "body of death" (Romans 7:24). The flesh will always remember its sins and try to be in charge. "If the Christian life looks too hard, we must remember that we are not called to live it by ourselves." One thing is certain: if a person has truly experienced conversion, sin will not and cannot hold him or her indefinitely.

Does Premarital Sex Equal Marriage?

I had a conversation with a person who was convinced that when a couple has sex, they are married in God's eyes. Their reasoning was that there were no marriage ceremonies in Bible days, and sex was the way people married. When I brought up the fact that Jesus performed his first miracle of turning water into wine during a marriage ceremony (John 2:1–11), they, like most people who choose to disobey God's commands, found an excuse to contradict this truth. They said it wasn't a marriage ceremony, but a celebration like a reception.

They went on to explain that Adam and Eve never had a marriage ceremony, and no such ceremonies are mentioned in the Bible for quite some time in the biblical record. And when you have sex with a person, you are at that moment married because the two souls are knit together. Today the marriage ceremony is just a formality and a piece of paper that a man came up with, once you have sex you are married to that person. They based their belief on 1 Corinthians 6:16 which says, *"do you not know that he who is joined to a harlot is one body with her? For "the two," He says,* "shall become one flesh."

I asked, "So, with that train of thought, what if you have, or have had multiple sexual partners? Does that mean that you are married to each partner? Have you now become a polygamist, or do you have to divorce each of these spouses that you married through sex? They said they were not tied to any one person they have had sex with in the past.

When I reminded her that God says sex outside marriage is fornication, they ignored that, and she had no explanation for the sexual sin of adultery. I left the conversation alone because this person had no real understanding of Scripture and wasn't willing to hear the truth according to Scripture. The Bible clearly says we are to "flee from sexual immorality" (Matthew 19:5-6, 1 Corinthians 6:18). This includes any kind of sexual activity apart from marriage.

Whether people agree with God or not, He says sex outside of marriage is fornication is sin and we should avoid it, flee from it. God says all sexual immorality a sin.

> "Flee from sexual immorality. Every other sin a person commits is outside the body, but the sexually immoral person sins against his own body." — 1 Corinthians 6:18 (ESV)

"For this is the will of God, your sanctification: that you abstain from sexual immorality;" — 1 Thessalonians 4:3 (ESV)

Proverbs 14:12 warns that *"There is a way that seems right to a man, but in the end, it leads to death."* From the perspective of Christian morality, what's so bad about having sex before you get married? Why did God rule it out? First of all God's plan for His children is good, not evil so everything He asks us to do is for our good.

Let's look at 1 Corinthians 6:16 again. In this passage, Paul Apostle is pointing out how big of a deal it is for them to be joined to a prostitute or to sleep with a prostitute. notice what Paul says about sleeping with a prostitute who's obviously not your wife. He says *Or do you not know that he who is joined to a prostitute becomes one body with her?* Genesis 2:24 says *Therefore a man shall leave his father and mother and be joined to his wife, and they shall become one flesh."*

One flesh doesn't mean those people are married it means that they have been joined, or connected but this is an ungodly connection and not a godly marriage. It's an ungodly union because it's outside of that bond of marriage that God instituted. In the Old and New Testament adultery does not equal polygamy and that's what would happen if sex equaled marriage.

Exodus 22:16-17 that helps us make this point even more clearly. *16 "If a man seduces a virgin who is not betrothed and lies with her, he shall give the bride-price for her and make her his wife. 17 If her father utterly refuses to give her to him, he shall pay money equal to the bride-price for virgins. (Exodus 22:16-17)* So from this passage we can see that even though they've slept together marriage and sex are two separate things. Notice that verse 17 says *if her father utterly refuses to give her to him, he shall pay money equal to the bride price.*

Even though the two have slept together, the father can say, "No. This is not a good match for marriage. It is not something I'll endorse, and so they don't get married even though they slept together." Can you see that, according to the Word sex and marriage are not the same thing? Rather, marriage is the holy place for sexual relationships. And outside of marriage, it becomes an ungodly thing, even though it is joining the two in some very real way, but not in the way of marriage.

We also see what Jesus says in John 4:17-18.

> "¹³ Jesus answered and said to her, "Whoever drinks of this water will thirst again, ¹⁴ but whoever drinks of the water that I shall give him will never thirst. But the water that I shall give him will become in him a fountain of water springing up into everlasting life." ¹⁵ The woman said to Him, "Sir, give me this water, that I may not thirst, nor come here to draw." ¹⁶ Jesus said to her, "Go, call your husband, and come here." ¹⁷ The woman answered and said, "I have no husband." Jesus said to her, "You have well said, 'I have no husband,' ¹⁸ for you have had five husbands, and the one whom you now have is not your husband; in that you spoke truly."

Jesus is speaking to a woman who has had a number of marriages, but the man she's with right now she's not married to. The woman said, "I have no husband." Jesus said to her "you are right in saying I have no husband" affirming that the man she's sleeping with is not her husband because sex does not equal marriage. One flesh in this passage is physical.

Soul Ties

> "But because of the temptation to sexual immorality, each man should have his own wife and each woman her own

husband." —*1 Corinthians 7:2 ESV*

Like the phrases 'the Trinity' and 'the rapture', you won't find the term "soul tie" in the Bible. However, each of these terms describes powerful truths that run throughout the scripture. The term "soul tie" means what it says. It's when two souls are tied together, joined together, or knit together to become one.

To understand "soul ties," we must understand the nature of man. When God made man, He made him to be a spirit, to have a soul, and to live in a body. As spiritual beings with a soul, living in a body, we were designed to interact and bond with God and one another in such a deep and wonderful way that the Bible describes us as being capable of being knit together. What an amazing ability God has given us to be able to bond with family, friends, and companions and be a blessing to one another! Most of these relationships form good godly bonds, good soul ties.

However, there can also be ungodly bonding, bad soul ties which can be formed in a variety of ways: physical, emotional, or verbal abuse, unforgiveness, sexual sin, domination, manipulation, abuse, and control are transmitted rather than blessings. An unhealthy soul tie could occur when an individual is unable to separate themselves from another person. They lose the ability to have their own interests, dreams, and friendships outside of the soul-tie relationship.

The Bible declares that in marriage God joins a husband and wife (Mark 10:8). Sexual union joins the two souls together as one flesh. Sex within marriage is an expression of love approved by God which makes marriage a good soul tie.

> *"So then, they are no longer two but one flesh. Therefore what God has joined together, let not man separate."* — Matthew 19:6

Divorce rips apart the knitting of souls that God created in marriage. This tearing of souls is why there is so much pain, sorrow, and trauma in divorce, and why God hates it.

A good soul tie can also be formed between a group of people with one common purpose. Scripture says, when the men of Israel gathered against the Tribe of Benjamin, they were knit together as one man (Judges 20:11).

A good soul tie can be formed between close friends, such as with Jonathan and David.

"By the time David had finished reporting to Saul, Jonathan was deeply impressed with David—an immediate bond was forged between them. He became totally committed to David. From that point on he would be David's number-one advocate and friend." —1 Samuel 18:1 (MSG)

Good soul ties can also be formed between brothers and sisters within the Body of Christ.

"that their hearts may be encouraged, being knit together in love, to reach all the riches of full assurance of understanding and the knowledge of God's mystery, which is Christ," — Colossians 2:2-3 (ESV)

"and not holding fast to the Head, from whom the whole body, nourished and knit together through its joints and ligaments, grows with a growth that is from God." —Colossians 2:19

Remember, sex joins you as one with another, so sex is not only physical; it is also emotional and spiritual. This means when you have sexual intercourse with someone, every part of you is involved. Your spirit, soul (mind, emotions, and will), and body are all involved. This is why when you break away, it hurts so bad; the souls have come together as one.

Genesis 34:2-3 gives us an excellent example of this:

"1-4 One day Dinah, the daughter Leah had given Jacob, went to visit some of the women in that country. Shechem, the son of Hamor the Hivite who was chieftain there, saw her and raped her. Then he felt a strong attraction to Dinah, Jacob's daughter, fell in love with her, and wooed her. Shechem went to his father Hamor, "Get me this girl for my wife." —Genesis 34:2-4 (MSG)

Notice that Shechem's soul cleaved unto Dinah even after he raped her. Rape or not, the same applies when you have sex with someone. Your soul cleaves to that person. You become one with the person you sleep with (1 Corinthians 6:16).

Domestic violence relationships are another good example of a bad soul tie. Have you ever met someone whose partner beats them or even has almost killed them, but instead of leaving, they just stayed, or if they did leave, they kept going back? What draws them back like a magnet to that abusive person?

Some signs of unhealthy soul ties include:

- Intense jealousy
- Possessiveness
- Codependency
- Anxiety when away from the other person
- Difficulty making decisions without the other person's input
- Struggling to define your identity without them

In the neighborhood where I lived as a teen, there was a couple who had been together for some time. They fought all the time, and the woman even shot the man several times, but he would not leave her or even press charges against her. I often wondered how he could keep going back to her. The answer is soul ties.

Angeline L. Williams

The Spirit of Sabotage

"The thief does not come except to steal, and to kill, and to destroy. I have come that they may have life, and that they may have it more abundantly." — John 10:10 NKJV

My earthly father was not around much when I was growing up, but I never doubted his love for me. The few times that he was around, he made a great impression upon me. Even as a young child, I realized that it was the addiction that prevented him from being a good father. I loved my dad, and I understood that he did the best he could. For years, I prayed for God to deliver and save him. God answered my prayer, delivered him, and saved him a year before he went home to the Lord.

One day, my dad looked at me with tears in his eyes and said, "I hope this spirit of sabotage that jumped on me has not gotten on you too." I didn't understand what he meant, but those words always stayed with me. For whatever reason, I had no real discernment of it until I began to pray about me and George's relationship.

> *Just because the enemy tries to stop it, does not mean he can thwart God's plan.*

As I looked back over my life, I noticed that whenever it seemed as if I was about to experience a breakthrough, something would happen to stop it. And every long-term romantic relationship I've ever been in pretty much ended the same way, for the same reason. As I prayed and listened, I also noticed some patterns at play in either my or George's lives. Ungodly beliefs regarding marriage, such as fear of commitment, previous relationship trauma, and the inability to have or keep a mate, were surface patterns that were revealed, along with other hindrances. The spirit of sabotage, the spirit of Pharaoh, strongholds, and soul ties were root issues that were brought to my attention.

Pharaoh, sabotage, and unholy strongholds have the same goal, which is to get you off course with God. My dad was on to something when he spoke about the spirit of sabotage. I believe it was the Spirit of God that spoke to him about this evil. The dictionary defines sabotage as "to deliberately destroy, damage, or obstruct (something), especially for political or military advantage." "Pharaoh" means the son of the sun.

The Egyptian kings were regarded as gods. The name Pharaoh has to do with the destruction of good things in their infancy. It was Pharaoh who gave the instruction that all male children of the Israelites must die because their increase in population posed a military threat to the Egyptians (Exodus 1:15-21). The assignment of the spirit of Pharaoh is to destroy destinies. Satan of course, was behind the scene attempting to thwart the plan of God.

Sabotage has been around for a very long-time attempting to destroy relationships and destinies. It was there in the Garden of Eden to destroy the relationship between man and God. Praise God for Jesus, God's Ram in the bush! It was sabotage who influenced Sanballat, Tobiah, Geshem, and the prophetess Noadiah to try to stop Nehemiah from rebuilding the walls of Jerusalem. It is sabotage who comes to try to stop us from completing the work of God.

Nehemiah was aware that this evil presence was at work, for he said:

"12 Then I perceived that God had not sent him at all, but

that he pronounced this prophecy against me because Tobiah and Sanballat had hired him. 13 For this reason he was hired, that I should be afraid and act that way and sin, so that they might have cause for an evil report, that they might reproach me." Nehemiah 6:12-13 (ESV)

As we can see, Sabotage tried to get Nehemiah to abort his mission. If someone is not paying attention and listening to God, Sabotage can convince them to abort divine directives, relationships, and destinies ordained by God. For instance, have you ever tried to press in deeper with God, and it seemed as if distractions popped up out of nowhere to derail you?

Has God ever asked you to do something, and as soon as you attempted to do it, all hell breaks loose against you? Suddenly, your finances take a huge hit, the kids start acting up, or lies and gossip are started about you. More than likely, you encountered the evil of Sabotage.

Sabotage works with familiar spirits who monitor your every move, informing it of your strengths, weaknesses, breaks in hedges of protection, and tendencies of both the perpetrator and the victim so it can launch an attack. Remember when Peter resisted Jesus' decision to return to Jerusalem because he knew He would be crucified? The to them who are the called according to his purpose." — Romans 8:28

"The angel of the LORD encamps around those who fear him, and he delivers them." — Psalm 34:7.

"Behold, I send an Angel before thee, to keep thee in the way, and to bring thee into the place which I have prepared." — Exodus 23:20.

"⁹ Two are better than one, because they have a good reward for their toil. ¹⁰ For if they fall, one will lift up his fellow. But woe to him who is alone when he falls and has not another to lift him up! ¹¹ Again, if two lie together, they keep warm, but how can one keep warm alone? ¹² And though a man might prevail against one who is alone, two will withstand him—a threefold cord is not quickly broken. — Ecclesiastes 4:9-12 primary purpose of Jesus' coming to earth was to be crucified, and Satan wanted to stop Him. Jesus didn't rebuke Peter.

He knew Satan was behind Peter's statement, and He went after the source. He turned to Peter and said, "Get behind me, Satan" (Matthew 16:23). Was Peter demon-possessed? Did he intend to be a stumbling block to Jesus? No, he did not. This all may sound far-fetched, but Satan's hierarchy is very organized, as Paul indicates in Ephesians 6:12.

God said regarding my engagement ending, "*An ener*[y] *has done this, pray.*" I believe sabotage was the ringle[ader] of the attack. I'm not sure why the devil is afraid of [the un]ion of George and I, but I do know that just becau[se the en]emy is uncomfortable, does not mean that he [is not in] the plan of God.

Again, if God does indeed intend for [us to] be together, He will do what He can to [bring us together]. In the meantime, I will stay connecte[d to God, walk in] my authority in Christ, and put th[e Word of God] on the situation:

> "No weapon formed agai[nst me shall prosper... my] heritage as children of [God...]

> "All things work tog[ether for good...]

Angeline L. Williams

Spiritual Strongholds

"For the weapons of our warfare are not of the flesh but have divine power to destroy strongholds." — 2 Corinthians 10:4 ESV

What is a stronghold? The dictionary defines it as a place that has been fortified so as to protect it against attack, and a place where a particular cause or belief is strongly defended or upheld. The word stronghold is also used as a metaphor for God's protection. Usually, when we hear the word "stronghold," it brings up images of evil spirits and the kingdom of darkness, which I refer to as an "unholy stronghold. We can also have what I call "Holy Strongholds" as well. We all have strongholds, holy and unholy.

Holy Strongholds

Psalm 18:2 reads, "The LORD is my rock and my fortress and my deliverer, my God, my rock, in whom I take refuge, my shield, and the horn of my salvation, my stronghold."

Jesus became our Stronghold at the Cross. He is a Shield, Deliverer, Protector, Fortress, Anchor and Refuge! For those who put their trust in Him, the LORD is a mighty fortress that we can run to when we are threatened by danger or tempted by sin. We can run to the LORD for protection against the enemy's advances and for restoration and strength from emotional weariness.

Our strength and protection do not depend on money, brick and stone, weapons, security systems, the absence of conflict, or a life free of trouble. No matter how great your security system is, if a thief wants in, he will find a way to get in. Money can buy things, but it cannot buy true and lasting peace. Put your trust in the LORD as our source of strength and security.

"2 And he said: "The Lord is my rock and my fortress and my deliverer; 3 The God of my strength, in whom I will trust; My shield and the horn of my salvation, My strong-

hold and my refuge; My Savior, You save me from violence." — *2 Samuel 22:2-3*

"The Lord is my light and my salvation; whom shall, I fear? The Lord is the stronghold of my life; of whom shall I be afraid?" —*Psalm 27:1*

In Nehemiah 8:10, David declares, "This day is holy to our Lord, and do not feel hurt, for the joy of Jehovah is your stronghold." Nahum 1:7 declares, "The LORD is good, a stronghold in the day of trouble; and He knows those who trust in Him." So, you see, to those who have faith in Him, God is a stronghold. He is a refuge, a fortress, and a stronghold against the troubles of this world. He offers protection and help to everyone who calls upon Him in faith.

Unholy Strongholds

Our Christian life follows the same pattern of Israel in the Old Testament. Like Israel, we all experience a new beginning, a time of deliverance from the world, a time of wandering in the wilderness learning how to live out our new life, times of testing, times of conquest, and times of refreshing. I explain this in the book "Put The Word In Your Mouth."

We've determined that we are in a spiritual war with the devil and his evil cohorts. No one is exempt. Trauma, rejection, hurt, anger, and disappointment affect us all. In addition to his constant harassment, temptations, and attacks, Satan seeks territories where he can establish unholy strongholds in which he can dominate and hold us captive. He searches for people, cities, and nations where he is not resisted, so he and his forces may flourish (1 Peter 5:8).

These "unholy strongholds" are Satan's primary tactics against humans. Let me point out that having an unholy stronghold does not mean that you are demon-possessed, evil, or that God can't use you. Every person has at least one unholy stronghold, even though they may not be aware of it.

While demons are actively involved in building them, an unholy stronghold is not a demon. This deception has even people who are aware of unholy strongholds fighting the wrong enemy. An unholy stronghold is a thought pattern based on lies and deception from the kingdom of darkness. An unholy stronghold is anything that sets itself up against the knowledge of God.

> *"The LORD is good, a stronghold in the day of trouble; and He knows those who trust in Him."* — Nahum 1:7

Strongholds originate in our thoughts and lead to belief systems. Satan builds fortresses around the mind in an attempt to control us, so that he can oppress, discourage, dictate, and influence how you view or react to situations, circumstances, or people at will. His goal is to put people into bondage and block us from the things of God. Once the fortress is built, he will defend it to the end. This is why Paul cautions us to demolish arguments and pretensions that set themselves up against the knowledge of God; to take every thought captive and make it obedient to Christ (2 Corinthians 10:5).

The word "imaginations" comes from the Greek word *logismos*, which is where we get the word "logic," as in "logical thinking." Your logical mind is carnal. The Greek word for carnal is *sarkikos*, which signifies having the nature of flesh, i.e., sensual, controlled by animal appetites, governed by human nature, instead of by the Spirit of God.

> *Your mind is your greatest asset, and the devil wants it.*

Romans 8:7 says the carnal mind is enmity against God: for it is not subject to the law of God, neither indeed can be. Your logical, carnal mind will always try to talk you out of obeying God. In fact, if you don't take charge of your mind, it will begin to completely dominate and control your obedience to God.

Thank God for giving us a sound mind, but even a sound mind must be submitted to the sanctifying work of the Holy Spirit. Otherwise, your mind will develop a stronghold of natural reasoning that starts to dictate all kinds of lies in your life.

Unholy strongholds can not only block your blessings, they can also convince you to walk away from your blessings. For instance, people say if it's God's will, it will happen; what God has for me is for me. But what about your free will that God will not override? What about the blessings and promises of God that you reject because of unbelief?

What about when you lean to your own understanding and reject God's plan and purpose? What about when you reject God's best because it doesn't look like you imagined?

> *Unholy strongholds can convince you to walk away from your blessings.*

Adam and Eve rejected God's purpose and ate of the forbidden tree (Genesis 3:1-6), and we are reaping the result of that today. The Pharisees and lawyers rejected God's counsel for themselves, not having been baptized by him (Luke 7:30).

Jesus wanted to gather the people of Jerusalem to himself, but they rejected their destiny, and their city was made desolate (Matthew 23:37-38). People reject Jesus Christ; the Jews rejected Jesus and cried for Him to be crucified. They cry out to God to bless them, and because the blessing doesn't look like what they imagined, they don't recognize it or accept it when it comes.

Are you rejecting the very thing you have been crying out to God for? Are you trying to kill the gift that God has brought to you? Yes, you have a choice. You can say "no" to the will and plan of God and go your own way, but if you reject God's will, you will surely miss the best God has for your life. At the end of the day, knowing but not doing God's will is like walking around with your left shoe on your right foot with the laces tied; it will trip you and cause you to stumble.

A marriage relationship is supposed to be a place where you feel safe with your spouse. Ephesians 5 instructs married couples to consistently demonstrate love, joy, faithfulness, goodness, gentleness, kindness, peace, and patience towards each other.

The marriage relationship should reflect Christ. Marital strongholds, sinful behaviors, or attitudes are contrary to Christ and need to be torn down. God knew that strongholds were at play in George and me when He reconnected us and exposed them, so apparently it was time for Him to deal with them. We just had to be willing to let him.

In 2 Corinthians chapter 10, Paul explains that unholy strongholds are presented as arguments, reasonings, and theories.

> *³ For though we walk (live) in the flesh, we are not carrying on our warfare according to the flesh and using mere human weapons. ⁴ For the weapons of our warfare are not physical [weapons of flesh and blood], but they are mighty before God for the overthrow and destruction of strongholds,*
>
> *⁵ [Inasmuch as we] refute arguments and theories and reasonings and every proud and lofty thing that sets itself up against the [true] knowledge of God; and we lead every thought and purpose away captive into the obedience of Christ (the Messiah, the Anointed One)* — 2 Corinthians 10:3-5 (AMPC)

Who presents these arguments, reasonings, and theories? Satan and his demons do. They work in the spiritual arena of your life trying to inject his lies into your mind, repeating them over and over until you start to think they are your thoughts. His goal is to build fortresses (strongholds) in your mind that he can use as a base of operations to attack you whenever he feels like it to bring confusion and chaos and undermine God's purposes for your life.

Satan and his demons have been monitoring you and your potential mate since you were born. They know your insecurities, weaknesses, and fears, and they use them to create circumstances that tempt you to sin. They know what thoughts to plant to agitate your emotions until you are too confused to resist and pray.

One of Satan's strong points is patience. He will invest the time it takes to destroy you. He looks for vulnerable areas, such as past failures, character weaknesses, and trauma, to plant deceptive thoughts. With couples, it may be suspicions and jealousy or thoughts to exaggerate each other's failures and inadequacies. It's all meant to steal your focus off of God and bring division and destruction. If you can remember all of this, you can notice when the enemy shows his hand and take authority.

> "The thief does not come except to steal, and to kill, and to destroy. I have come that they may have life, and that they may have it more abundantly" — John 10:10 NKJV

Satan wants us to wrestle with the "symptom" rather

than the "source," so he disguises his activities, so it appears as if someone or something else is to blame for the strife and chaos going on in our lives. Like cold medicine, which doesn't cure a cold and only relieves the symptoms; you can fight the symptoms of the devil, but you will not end the problem until you deal with the source and bind the "strong man."

> *You can fight the symptoms, but you will not end the problem until you deal with the source.*

Satan has been using this strategy for a long time. When Jesus was on earth, Satan attempted to build strongholds in His mind too, so that he could influence his thoughts and direct his actions. After Jesus had been fasting for 40 days, Satan tried to get Jesus to use human reasoning to deal with his weakness. Even in His weakness, Jesus was aware of who He was and what Satan was up to. He used His Sword! He used the Word of God to combat all the devil's temptations, and he left him.

Satan planted the thought in Ananias and Sapphira's hearts to lie in Acts 5:3. He gave them the idea to sell a piece of property, give some of the money to the church, and then pretend that they had given the full amount. Peter asked Ananias, "Why has Satan filled your heart to lie to the Holy Spirit?" Carrying out this thought cost them their lives.

Satan planted thoughts into King David's mind. 1st Chronicles 21:1 says, "Then Satan stood up against Israel and moved David to number Israel." Satan gave David the thought to start counting to see exactly how strong the nation really was. Thinking this was his own idea, David decided to take a census. Taking this census was a sin because it showed that David was relying on human strength rather than depending on God, and God judged an entire nation for David's sin. Satan planted the thought to betray Jesus into Judas' heart (mind) (John 13:2). So please don't think that you are a match for him without Christ and the power of the Holy Spirit.

When you entertain thoughts and participate in activities contrary to the will of God, you open yourself up to demonic influence. You are choosing to walk by the flesh rather than walk in faith and in obedience. I thank God for His mercy and the blood of Jesus, which covers our sin, because I have succumbed to Satan's tactics many times, but God honored His word and protected me in spite of me. Which is why I know that it is important to understand what unholy strongholds are, where they come from, and how to be rid of them. As I continued to pray and listen, God reminded me of some things I thought, said, and did in my relationship with George. Even though I am consciously working on changing my thoughts and speech from what He taught me when I wrote the book "Put The Word in Your Mouth."

I hadn't been in a romantic relationship in so long that I did not know that these strongholds were there, but God did. Satan used grief, loneliness, and other lies to attempt to stop me from moving forward in God, but I kept moving, praying for and encouraging others in the midst of my own tears. He knew I desired to be remarried and he tried to tell me that I was going to grow old alone, that no one would ever love me, that no man is going to want me with disfigured breasts.

The lies just kept coming and replaying in my head. Then here comes this tall and gorgeous man who was just as broken as I was, and I opened up my heart to him. I'm not saying that Satan sent George to hurt me because I don't believe that. I believe God brought us together for His purpose. I also believe that because of all that I was dealing with within myself, I built George up as a knight in shining armor who was going to make everything all right. Listen, God can use people to bring deliverance, but no person can be your savior.

As the replay played out on the screen of my mind, I could see that because of my insecurities I trusted ME, MYSELF, AND I, instead of God with the relationship. God showed me how I listened to Satan's lies, even when He told me to stop and take a breath, I talked to myself saying all sorts of things that undermined the relationship.

I have never been good at hiding what I feel, so probably most of what I was feeling came out in my actions. God showed me that I made evil assumptions about George. The truth is, George told me and showed me nearly every day that he loved me. He made sure that my needs were met, and I wasn't even his wife yet.

When he spoke of the future, he used words like "us" and "we" rather than "I." He got down on one knee and asked me to marry him. Despite all George did, I was anxious and worried, and subconsciously tried to make things go the way I wanted them to go. I tried to rush the process.

"My God, I cried out. I'm so sorry." I repented and prayed for George and myself, and I apologized to George. Can you see how Satan's fortresses of lies can influence every area of your life? Fortresses of fear of abandonment and insecurity had been building up in me since I was a child, and they got stronger during my previous marriage. I thought, because I had forgiven my ex-husband, that all was well!

I thank God for using George to bring my issues to the surface. Like I have done since I gave my life to the Lord years ago, I am allowing God to deliver me. I pray George is doing the same. He is a long way from perfect, but he is an amazing man. No matter what happens, I choose to see him through God's eyes, as a mighty man of God delivered and set free. He whom the Lord sets free is free indeed.

I don't know how things will work out with us, but I trust that God will work everything for our good, whether we are together or apart. I believe if God indeed brought us together to be husband and wife, He will do what He can to make that happen.

Identifying Unholy Strongholds

There are hundreds of unholy strongholds which can exist in people lives. We can recognize that an unholy stronghold exists when we see destructive habits, or behavioral patterns, repetitive negative thoughts and behaviors that you have no control over; you feel compelled to do things you constantly do things that you even you don't approve of, or which is against your own will.

Following are some internal fruits produced by unholy strongholds:

- Chronic worry, feelings of insecurities, guilt, shame, anxieties, bitterness, resentment,
- Judging and condemning yourself and/or others.
- Feelings of powerlessness over anger, fear, stress and depression, and the ability to deny the truth.
- Low self-worth, unbelief, ungodly thoughts and many more.
- Rejection and seeking the approval of others.

Some external fruits of unholy strongholds are:
- Impulsive, obsessive, and compulsive behavior.

- Broken relationships.
  Fear of letting anyone to close.

- Gossiping

- Recycling bad habits, and addictions.

- Stubborn will; unteachable; will not take correction; refuses to submit to authority.

- Prideful, arrogant, defensive, controlling, and manipulative.

The origin of a stronghold usually starts within our childhood. Brick-by-brick Satan uses past experiences to establish "unholy strongholds" in our hearts and lives by repeatedly implanting lies in us about God and about us. He also uses negative childhood memories to build destructive patterns in our lives.

Children who grow up in an abusive environment can also become abusers; a child who grows up around alcohol or drug abuse will grow up repeating the same pattern themselves, even though they may have hated their home environment. This happens because of a stronghold that has been established.

For example, if Satan wants to destroy your concept of

love and build up a stronghold of self-hatred, low self-esteem, and low self-confidence, he will use people to say things to you like:

- You'll never be good enough.
- You can't do anything right. You are a failure.
- You are ugly, you are stupid.
- You're worthless, nobody loves you.
- You'll never be good enough.
- You're no good just like your daddy.
- You are no good just like your momma.

These are just a few of the lies that the enemy uses to disrupt your thought life. Years of hearing such lies grow deeply into our hearts, taking root, distorting your self-image, and causing you to agree with and repeat them. You may start forming patterns of behavior that often remain unnoticed until the damage has been done, or until God reveals them to you. Sometimes, even when we do notice it, instead of trying to get free, we cover it up. My ex-husband, for instance, had a lying stronghold. Some people will tell a lie to get something, to get out of trouble, or to keep from hurting someone's feelings, but he just lied for no reason.

Once when I called him on one of his lies, he said he was taught that if he told a lie, he must take that lie to his grave. He must never recant it and tell the truth. That could have been a lie too, but he lived by that philosophy, and he would defend his lies to the end. It became impossible for me to trust him.

Unholy strongholds play a big part in how we act and feel, and how we respond to various situations in life. They can also lie dormant in our soul until Satan decides to use them to block us, or God wants to free you from it and then it will surface.

Whether negative or positive, we will act out and fulfill what is constantly spoken into our belief system. If you constantly think you are a failure, you will feel and act like a failure, and eventually, you will begin to give up before trying. If you have not forgiven yourself for past mistakes, you will believe and act like you don't deserve good to come to you.

Some years ago, I was with a grandmother and her granddaughter. The child was around five or six. I listened to the grandmother talk about the child's behavior, and as she did, the child began to act out just what the grandmother was saying. When I brought it to her attention, she yelled at me and told me to mind my own business. This is an example of how we will act out and react to the words we constantly hear.

People try to change their actions and behavior, block bad memories, and push evil thoughts out of their head with things and substances, only to end up in deeper captivity. A makeover won't do it, a new car, drugs and alcohol, more money, or sex won't do it. They will only camouflage what's really in your heart.

Scripture says it is the truth that makes us free (John 8:32). Until you change what you are hearing and replace the lie with the truth of God's Word, you will not be free. You must cast down the lie and replace it with the truth of God's Word, or you won't be able to receive God's best for you. Speaking faith-filled words is God's way to bring things into existence, so speak the promise, not the problem.

The pastor can lay hands on you and pray a thousand prayers, but if you don't believe the words of the prayer, they are just going in one ear and out the other. In order to receive from God, you must believe and receive His promises.

"And without faith it is impossible to please him, for whoever would draw near to God must believe that he exists

and that he rewards those who seek him."— Hebrews 11:6 (ESV)

Faith, whether positive or negative, comes by hearing. A person won't believe they are unattractive until someone calls them ugly. A person doesn't believe they are worthless until someone says they are worthless. As a man thinks in his heart, so is he. If you believe you are unlovable, it will prevent you from receiving love from others until you change your belief. If you know your sins are forgiven, Satan won't be able to bind you in condemnation. If you think about the fact that you have been washed clean by the blood of Jesus, you will feel clean inside.

The Word of God has much to say about how much we are loved and valued by God. You can begin to tear down those lies of unworthiness and unlovable right now. Here are some truths that God says about you. Read them aloud, and let your spirit man hear them. Read and memorize them until you can say them when the lies pop up:

1. *"But God demonstrates His own love toward us, in that while we were still sinners, Christ died for us" (Romans 5:8).* God loves you so much that He allowed His only begotten Son to die in your place before you ever thought about repenting.

2. *"Therefore, if anyone is in Christ, he is a new creation; old things have passed away; behold, all things have become new" (2 Corinthians 5:17).* If you belong to Jesus, you have a brand new, blood washed clean life in Him. Old things have passed away; behold, all things have become new

3. *"Behold what manner of love the Father has bestowed on us, that we should be called children of God!" (1 John 3:1).* God considers you His very own precious child. Isn't that amazing?

4. *"Knowing that you were not redeemed with corruptible things, like silver or gold ... but with the precious blood of Christ" (1 Peter 1:18, 19).* God was willing to pay the highest price to redeem you—the blood of His dear Son. That says a lot about how valuable you are to God!

5. *"Now then, we are ambassadors for Christ, as though God were pleading through us" (2 Corinthians 5:20).* God thinks so much of you that He has given you a high calling as an Ambassador to share His great love with others.

In 2nd Corinthians 10:5, we are told to cast down imaginations. Imaginations are simply things that we imagine.

The enemy usually plants them in our minds with questions, like he did with Eve and attempted to do with Christ. Don't waste your time trying to reason with the devil. Cast down the imagination and throw it out! Any thought that is not cast down and brought into subjection to the Word of God will begin to build a stronghold in the mind.

> *³ For though we walk in the flesh, we do not war according to the flesh. ⁴ For the weapons of our warfare are not carnal but mighty in God for pulling down strongholds, ⁵ casting down arguments and every high thing that exalts itself against the knowledge of God, bringing every thought into captivity to the obedience of Christ, — 2 Corinthians 10:3-5 (NKJV)*

There are two primary unholy strongholds. Every lie Satan uses to build strongholds in our mind are rooted in two lies:

1. an incorrect perception of God, and
2. an incorrect perception of who we are

Incorrect Perception of Who We?

People who deal with this stronghold are caught up in shame-based thinking. They have a tough time seeing themselves as new person in Christ Jesus. They deal with constant guilt and condemnation and lack spiritual confidence because they don't understand what Christ has done on the Cross and how it applies to their own life. They do not realize that it's God's will and it is good for them to disassociate themselves from their past.

Incorrect Perception of God

One of Satan's biggest lies that he uses against believers and unbelievers is an incorrect perception of God. People troubled by this stronghold see God as a cruel and unloving dictator who plays favorites, rather than a loving Father who sent His only begotten Son to die for their sin.

This stronghold keeps nonbelievers from coming to God. It keeps believers in a never-ending cycle of self-righteousness, and performance-based religion. These believers try to live up to the impossible rules and regulations of The Law that only served to solidify the need for Jesus' sacrifice at the Cross.

People bound by this stronghold tend to think doing right equals being righteousness. However, that is not true:

> "...for if righteousness come by the law, then Christ is dead in vain." — Galatians 2:21

Many are so scared of being 'outside' of God's will, that being a Christian seems like a chore rather than a blessing. If we are trying to keep the rituals, rules, and regulations of The Law, then we negate what Christ has done at the Cross. Galatians 5:4 states it this way:

> "Christ is become of no effect unto you, whosoever of you are justified by the law; ye are fallen from grace."

I'm not saying we are to live willy-nilly and do whatever we want, because we know what's right and what's wrong. Scripture says to know to do right and not do it is sin (James 4:17).

If you recognize that you are dealing with this stronghold, accept that if you have believed on Jesus you are in right standing with God right now, regardless of what you did yesterday or even earlier today. You didn't shock or surprise God with it, so release it, repent, and ask God to forgive you and help you not to do it again and keep moving forward. God is not condemning you, so don't you condemn yourself, and certainly don't allow the accuser the devil to condemn you. Begin to pray with confident faith for God to lead and use You for His glory.

I'm reminded of the woman with the issue of blood

who had been bound in her body and her mind for 12 years (Matthew 9:20-22). For 12 long years that sickness spoke to her telling her that this was her fate, but one day she *heard* about a man named Jesus who was going about healing all manner of disease. Faith rose up and the voice inside her head changed.

She cast down those evil imaginations that kept telling her that she was going to die, and she replaced it with the Truth. She kept saying as she reached out for Jesus, "If I can just touch his robe, I will be healed." She said it over, and over and over again "If I can just touch his robe, I will be healed." And when she just touched the hem of his garment Jesus said, "Daughter, be of good comfort; thy faith hath made thee whole."

When you are trying to drive stinkin-thinkin out of your mind you can do it by saying the promise over and over until that stinkin-thinkin is gone!

Unholy Stronghold Examples

Example 1: A young man lived a pretty rough life, then he accepted Christ's sacrifice on the Cross and gave his life to God. He asked God to forgive him, but he was so focused on his past mistakes that he didn't feel free. He believed that he had to confess all his sins to everyone he has ever wronged, so he could be forgiven. He remembered a few people and went to them to confess his sins.

Some forgave him for what he'd done to them, but most just yelled at him because they couldn't forgive him. He couldn't find some people, and a couple had died, so he couldn't confess to them. He felt awful and guiltier than before he started. He felt like a failure, even though God has forgiven him, and the Blood of Jesus has washed away all his past mistakes and failures and cast them into the sea of forgetfulness!

Example 2: A young lady was physically abused by her drug addicted mother who never gave her attention, or affection and never appreciated her or acknowledged her achievements. She was molested and raped over and over and by the age of 14 she was a broken. She lost her self-esteem and saw herself as a loser and thought her life was worthless. All of this led to drug addiction and everything that comes with that life. A friend ministers the love of Christ, but she can't receive because she can't forgive the wrong that was done to her, and she can't forgive herself for the wrong that she has done.

Example 3: A young man gets married and cheats on

his wife, and they divorce. He marries again, but he is now addicted to crack cocaine. His wife gets tired of his habit and divorces him. God delivers him, and he gets his life back on track. He gets married again for the third time, but he is so bitter and unforgiving that his new wife can't handle it and divorces him too. He meets a wonderful woman and wants to marry again, but the devil tells him that she will treat him just like the other wives. It is not true, but he believes it, so he walks away based on the lies Satan has built up in his mind.

Example 4: You spend much of your time focused on discussing the faults of family and friends. You delight in hearing and spreading gossip and you find yourself constantly on the phone trying to get information about others.

Are you getting an idea of how destructive strongholds are in your life and how they can hurt your relationships? Can you see why you must diligently pursue deliverance?

Angeline L. Williams

Getting Free

"See, I have this day set thee over the nations and over the kingdoms, to root out, and to pull down, and to destroy, and to throw down, to build and to plant" — *Jeremiah 1:10*

In God's eyes, believers are new creatures, made perfect and complete at salvation (2 Corinthians 5:17). We are delivered from the power and bondage of sin; however, we are not changed into perfect beings that never sin.

We are also empowered with the tools to war against our own strongholds of sin, but it up to us to learn how to use the tools. You are going to need help to do this. No Christian is called to walk this Christian journey alone. God tells us in His Word not to neglect to meet together (Hebrews 10:25).

Even if you study the Bible on your own, you are commanded to gather with other believers to hear and study the Scriptures and worship Jesus. The most common way to gather is to go to church. Gathering with other believers is a refining process where we help each other, pray for each other, and encourage each other.

Jesus said, "Where two or three are gathered in my name, there am I among them" (Matthew 18:20). So, Jesus not only lives in us by His Spirit, but He is in the "midst" of us when we gather to worship Him. If you are not a part of a Bible-believing fellowship that you attend regularly, I encourage you to seek God about this.

We all struggle with strongholds of sin, things that we can't seem to get victory over either because of lack of knowledge and or disobedience. Many times, we are taught to cast out strongholds, but Paul tells us in 2nd Corinthians 10:3-5 that we must pull them down and destroy them!

As I have stated several times, since strongholds and everything else Satan does is built upon deception and lies, the only way to counter them is with the truth. Where do we find the truth? In the Word of God. You can huff and puff, kick and scream all you want, but the stronghold will only build up power from the friction and the strife.

You can't holler and scream at people to get them to see that they have strongholds. They will just put up their defensive walls and reject you. Until you bring the truth of God's Word on the scene, nothing will change. It's the Word of God that brings deliverance.

> *⁸ Seek him that maketh the seven stars and Orion, and turneth the shadow of death into the morning, and maketh the day dark with night: that calleth for the waters of the sea, and poureth them out upon the face of the earth: The Lord is his name: ⁹ That strengtheneth the spoiled against the strong, so that the spoiled shall come against the fortress. — Amos 5:8-9 (KJV)*

Remember restoration is God's work, but we must yield to His work in us. Pride will keep you from seeing things about yourself and keep you focused on how the "other person" needs to change.

I was instructed to intercede for George, but God also showed me what was holding me captive. I had to recognize and acknowledge my own destructive behavior and then yield to God so that He could deliver in me. I am still a work in progress.

To break free from any bondage of Satan whether it is a stronghold, a soul tie, or a spirit of sabotage to be free from we need to shut the door to Satan. How do we shut the door to Satan?

Whatever it might be, you must first see that there is a problem and acknowledge it. If you can't see it, you won't acknowledge it. Proverbs 28:13 tells us, "He who covers his sins will not prosper, but whoever confesses and forsakes them will have mercy." We must acknowledge our sin, repent and ask God to forgive us and cleanse us from all unrighteousness. (Psalms 32, 1 John 1:9).

David prayed, "Examine me, O Lord, and prove me; try my mind and my heart." Ask God to reveal any strongholds in your life. You can pray the following scripture:

> *"23 Search me, O God, and know my heart: try me, and know my thoughts: 24 And see if there be any wicked way in me, and lead me in the way everlasting." — Psalm 139:23-24 (KJV)*

Be humble and honest before God, and let the Holy Spirit expose the darkness. God may or may not answer right away, so be patient. Continue to praise and pray. If God leads you to fast, do so. When He reveals the strongholds in your life, acknowledge them and repent. Then go to the Word of God and meditate on and study the opposite truth from God.

Unforgiveness and Bitterness

Unforgiveness and bitterness are the number-one ways the enemy gains access to attack you. Unforgiveness and bitterness are chains that imprison us and hinder our relationship with God. In this fallen world we live in, we will face hurt and offense, and more than likely, it is the people closest to us that hurt us the most. People's words, actions, and inactions can wound us to the core and can cause bitterness and resentment to take root in our hearts. Choosing to hold on to bitterness and resentment and refuse to forgive opens the door wide open for the enemy to attack Christians. Many believe some offenses are so bad they can't forgive, probably because they don't understand what forgiveness is.

If you struggle to forgive, understand that forgiving is not forgetting! The Lord never said you have to forget, but He did say we are to forgive. It's not a suggestion. It is a command. You may say or feel like you can never forgive, but if you are honest, you don't want to forgive. The truth is, you can forgive with the Lord's help. If it were impossible, God wouldn't have commanded us to forgive.

Also, forgiveness is not saying that what they did or what happened was okay. It wasn't. What happened, what was said was not okay, but let God handle it, release forgiveness toward them, and close the door of unforgiveness.

Here is a prayer you can pray regarding unforgiveness:

Heavenly Father, I come to You today for help. I know I

need to forgive _____ (name the person). Please give me the strength to fully forgive him/her. Help me do this from the bottom of my heart – without any reservation or condition. To You I surrender all the bitterness, hostility, and hatred I have held towards him/her. Father, I ask You to forgive them for what they have done. Heal me as You lead me to live in complete freedom in Christ (Galatians 5:1). Thank You for hearing my prayer. I am grateful for Your patience and everlasting love. In Jesus' name I pray, amen."

Wield Your Sword

The Sword of the Spirit is the Word of God (Ephesians 6:12). Many believers do not use it as effectively as they should. Satan and his demons are not omnipresent, neither can they read our minds.

Remember, I said Satan and his demons have been monitoring you since you were born. They know so much about us because they hear what we speak, what is spoken over us and they see our actions. They can plant thoughts, but they do not know our thoughts, so we must speak out loud to interact with them.

This is what Jesus did when Satan came to tempt Him in Matthew 4. Jesus was showing us how to use the Word as a sword. To use the Word as a sword against the enemy, you must declare the Word to him!

Say God reveals to you that a stronghold of fear has been hindering your growth and affecting your relationships. You can whip out the Sword (scriptures on freedom from fear, freedom in Christ) and speak to those tormenting spirits. You can speak them directly to the spirit of fear like Jesus spoke directly to the fig tree (Mark 11:12-25):

You can confess:

"God has not given me a spirit of fear, but of love, power, and a sound mind" (2 Timothy 1:7).

There is no fear in love; but perfect love casts out fear. I have been made perfect in love. (1 John 4:18) You spirit of fear, you get out of here, in Jesus' Name!"

The LORD is my light and my salvation; Whom shall I fear? The LORD is the strength of my life; Of whom shall I be afraid? (Psalms 27:1 NKJV)

³ Though an army may encamp against me, My heart shall not fear; Though war may rise against me, In this I will be confident. ⁴ One thing I have desired of the LORD, That will I seek: That I may dwell in the house of the LORD All the days of my life, to behold the beauty of the LORD, And to inquire in His temple. ⁵ For in the time of trouble He shall hide me in His pavilion; In the secret place of His tabernacle He shall hide me; He shall set me high upon a rock.

> ⁶*And now my head shall be lifted up above my enemies all around me; Therefore I will offer sacrifices of joy in His tabernacle; I will sing, yes, I will sing praises to the LORD. (Psalms 27:3-6 NKJV)*

As you do this, you are fortifying your spirit man and replacing those lies and tearing down that stronghold with truths! Keep in mind, the lie has been speaking to you for years, so it may not leave without a fight. You are going to have to be like the lady with the issue of blood and confess the truth over and over until it becomes like second nature to you.

A good scripture to consistently pray over your life is Psalm 144:1: *"Blessed be the Lord my strength, who prepares my hands for war, and my fingers to fight."*

Confess, believe, and count on God to give you the strategy to gain victory over whatever stronghold He reveals to you. Say the stronghold is rejection. You might begin to study and confess scriptures about God's acceptance such as:

> **Psalm 27:10**: *When my father and my mother forsake me, Then the Lord will take care of me. (NKJV)*

> **1 John 3:1**: *Behold what manner of love the Father has bestowed on us, that we should be called children of God! Therefore the world does not know us, because it did not*

know Him. (NKJV)

Romans 8:38-39: *"[38] For I am persuaded that neither death nor life, nor angels nor principalities nor powers, nor things present nor things to come, [39] nor height nor depth, nor any other created thing, shall be able to separate us from the love of God which is in Christ Jesus our Lord." (NKJV)*

Praise is a powerful weapon. Surround the stronghold with praise, singing psalms and spiritual songs to God. Put the Word in your mouth! Be confident and bold. You have the victory, and the gates of hell will not prevail against you as you advance in faith and not fear!

Praying and declaring God's words back to Him, is a powerful weapon against the forces of evil. Truth going out. It reminds us that God knows our way and understands what we face today. It builds our faith and our trust in God. It guards our hearts and focuses our minds back on Him. It wins the battle.

Prayer Of Repentance

Father God, I come before You in the Name of Jesus Christ. Thank You for the finished work of Jesus Christ that has empowered me to continually triumph over all the forces of evil. Your Word says that all who call upon the name of the Lord shall be saved. I claim that promise for myself today in Jesus' name.

I confess that I have participated in illegitimate sexual activities that are outside of Your will for my life. I acknowledge this is sin, and I ask Your forgiveness for yielding my body as an instrument of sin. I repent for the illegitimate sexual activities with _____ (*name each sexual partner*). I ask you to forgive me, take this sin, and put it on the cross, never to be held against me again. And Father, in the name of Jesus, I renounce the covenant I made with _____ (name each one). I choose to walk away from this lifestyle and behavior, and I renounce it from my life. Anything bad that came in through that covenant, I ask You to take it from me now, in Jesus' name. Thank you, Amen.

Prayer Against Marital Delay

Heavenly Father, You are the Righteous Judge of heaven and earth that is seated on the throne. I stand in Your presence under the covering of the blood of Jesus and under the covering and the covenant of your love for me (Psalm 86:5, Ephesians 2:4-5).

I acknowledge that I have sinned, particularly the sins of sexual immorality. I ask Father for Your forgiveness of all my sins, transgressions, and iniquities that have given my adversary legal grounds against me and my generational bloodline. In humility, I repent today, and I ask for Your forgiveness in the name of Your Son Jesus Christ, my Savior. I thank You, Father, for Your forgiveness and for cleansing me from the sins, transgressions, and iniquities, in the name of Jesus Christ, and for giving me the verdict, "Not guilty!"

Father, equip me and my future spouse in the mind, soul, and spirit with everything we need to have to be united with my life partner. Remove all obstacles that are blocking us from coming together. Deliver us from everything blocking us and standing against our beautiful marriage in Jesus' name. Thank You for fulfilling the desires of our hearts.

Now, Father, by the authority You have given me in the name of Jesus; I sever all soul ties, vows, pacts, evil covenants, or legal rights that came in because of the sin. Halleluiah Father! I am free. Your Word says whoever the Son of God sets free is free, indeed, and I have been set free through the blood of Jesus.

Declaration: The Word of God says that though the mountains be shaken, and the hills be removed, yet God's unfailing love for me will not be shaken, nor will His covenant of peace be removed. I declare that this promise of

God's love and compassion for me will be manifested in the area of marriage and in all areas of my life (Isaiah 54:10). I now seal my prayers with the blood of Jesus Christ.

Angeline L. Williams

Standing in The Gap

"Therefore I tell you, whatever you ask in prayer, believe that you have received it, and it will be yours." —Mark 11:24 ESV

For years God has called me to intercede or stand in the gap for others. I've seen Him do miraculous things in my life and in the life of others as a result of my obedience, so to me, this was no different. I believe I have been standing in the gap praying for my husband for years now.

It was June 11, 2014, when I had the dream of a man wandering in the wilderness. I remember the date because I write my dreams and Rhema words given to me by God in a journal with the date. I encourage you to document your spiritual encounters. If you are not journaling, I encourage you to start.

God often gives me instructions during the night hour,

I Don't Believe in Fairytales

I guess because my mind is still when I sleep. On this night I dreamed of a man standing in what seemed like the wilderness or desert. He was alone and dressed in dusty clothes that looked worn and tattered. The area around him was desolate, but it had bits of green shrubbery scattered about which I somehow knew symbolized life. I could not see his face clearly; I could only see his form. He was tall, around 6'3 or 6'4. I remember marveling at his long legs. Even though I couldn't see his face clearly, I sensed that I knew him. So, I kept trying to focus to see his face.

He was walking towards me and I thought to myself, okay I can see who this is now. Then he stopped and looked around like he was at a crossroad trying to figure out which direction to go in. I tried again to zoom in to see who he was because I really felt like I knew him, but I could still only see his tall silhouette. As I zoomed in, I heard a loud voice say, "husband, pray". Then I woke up.

When I woke up, I sought the Lord on what this dream meant. Again, I only heard the words, "husband, pray." So that is what I have been doing for a few years now. For a while I fervently prayed for this tall man in my dream, then I slowed down, but God has brought the dream back to my remembrance from time to time, or the thought of my future husband comes to mind, and I pray for him.

It's had been a while since I've thought about the dream. I didn't even remember it when George and I reconnected. Then all of a sudden as I'm writing this book the dream comes to mind and I realize that George actually fits build of the man in the dream. Now I am not saying that he is the guy, only God knows. I don't know who the man in the dream is, but I do know he was not my ex-husband, because at the time we were divorced, and he had remarried, and this man was much taller. Whoever this man is, I believe God wants me to pray for him, and I am confident that God's plan and purpose will be done in his life.

God wants all His children to stand in the gap for our families, churches, communities, the nation, and the lost, so it is important to understand what it means to "stand in the gap" or to "intercede" for others, and how to do it.

The word "intercede" comes from the Latin words "inter" which means "between" and "cedere" which means "go." An intercessor is someone who acts as a go-between, pleading to God on behalf of others. Jesus acted as our go-between on the Cross, and He continues to intercede for us from The Throne of Grace. Intercession is an ongoing work of Christ our High Priest.

> *"He is able to save forever those who draw near to God through him, because he always lives to make intercession for them"* — Hebrews 7:25.

> *"First of all, then, I urge that supplications, prayers, intercessions, and thanksgivings be made for all people ... This is good, and it is pleasing in the sight of God our Savior, who desires all people to be saved and to come to the knowledge of the truth."* — 1 Timothy 2:1; 3-4

To "stand in the gap" or "intercede" literally means "go between" or intervene on behalf of another. The idea of "standing in the gap" comes from Ezekiel 22:30 where God says,

> *"I looked for someone among them who would build up the wall and stand before me in the gap on behalf of the land, so I would not have to destroy it, but I found no one."* Ezekiel 22:40

Did you catch that? God said I looked for someone among them who would build up the wall and stand before me in the gap on behalf of the land *so that He would not have to destroy the land.* Jesus teaches us that it is necessary to ask before we receive, to seek before we find, and to knock before the door will be opened (Luke 11:9). Paul urges us in 1st Thessalonians 5:17 to pray without ceasing. God is willing and able to give us everything He wants to bless us with, but He chooses to wait until we ask, until we seek, and until we knock.

Intercession, like all prayer, takes place in the spiritual world where the battles for our soul, our lives, our families, our friends, and our nation are fought. Intercession is warfare. It involves commitment and perseverance. It is praying God's will on behalf of others and refusing to let go until His will comes to pass in their life. I interceded for my parents to be saved and delivered for years. It took some time, but God answered my prayer. I've seen God perform many miracles because of intercession.

Usually, when God has called me to stand in the gap for someone, He gives me specific insights, prophetic revelation, and scriptures to pray about and stand on. This is interesting because when George and I reconnected God revealed specific things for me to intercede for on behalf of George. I started praying according to what God showed me. I'm sure that played a part in why the enemy attacked our relationship the way he did.

Have you ever prayed for someone, and they just went berserk, and seemed to get worse? Maybe they even began to treat you like an enemy. When you see this happening don't stop praying. In fact, increase your praying. I know that it may hurt, but remember the real culprit is Satan and his evil forces, not the person.

Satan doesn't want to let go of those we intercede for, so he tries to convince you that your prayers are not being heard. He knows the fervent prayers of the righteous are powerful. He wants you to question God's ability to deliver, set free, and heal the person you are praying for.

We've all been there, but keep in mind what the living and active word says in Isaiah chapter 40:

> "*28 Have you not known? Have you not heard? The everlasting God, the Lord, The Creator of the ends of the earth, neither faints nor is weary. His understanding is unsearchable. 29 He gives power to the weak, and to those who have no might He increases strength. 30 Even the youths shall faint and be weary, and the young men shall utterly fall, 31 but those who wait on the Lord shall renew their strength; they shall mount up with wings like eagles, they shall run and not be weary, they shall walk and not faint."* — Isaiah 40:28-31

No matter how things look on the surface remember when we reach the end of our strength, our Father is right there to strengthen us. If God says keep going, then keep going. Be encouraged. It's not over until God says it's over.

Soulish Prayers

"And when you pray, do not heap up empty phrases as the Gentiles do, for they think that they will be heard for their many words." — Matthew 6:7 ESV

The soul is that carnal part of humans that wages war against the Spirit of God. The soul also known as flesh is the mind, the will, and the emotions. Our mind and soul are not capable of knowing the things of God, neither are our souls. Only our spirits can.

God does not answer prayers outside His will or prayers in agreement with Satan's desires.

Soulish prayer is prayer dictated by the prayer's emotions, will, or mind. Spirit-led prayer is praying the heart, the will, and the mind of the Father. God does not answer prayers outside His will or prayers in agreement with Satan's desires.

James 4:3 says, "Ye ask, and receive not, because ye ask

amiss, that ye may consume it upon your lusts."

Proverbs 18:21 says death and life are in the power of the tongue. This means the words we speak and pray, good or bad are powerful. Psalm 103:20 says that angels are "heeding the voice of God's word." So, who gives voice to God's Word? We do when we speak His Word!

> *Prayer is not a way to get God to do what we want Him to do, or to get other people to do what we want them to do.*

Many people think since God does not answer our amiss prayers that no harm is done. This can be true; however, like the angels of God heed the voice of His Word, Satan, and his imps use our negative words and actions to create havoc. With our very own mouths, we can give the devil a foothold to create havoc in our life and cause problems for others.

Prayer is not a way to get God to do what we want Him to do, or to get other people to do what we want them to do. We should never approach God praying our will. We should always pray His will. The best way to do that is to pray His Word, which contains His will.

Years ago, some people from a nearby church came

through my apartment complex witnessing. When I answered the door, they asked if they could pray for me. I said yes and shared what I wanted prayer for, then let them in, so they could pray. Well, when they came in, they saw an ashtray on the coffee table and asked if I smoked. I said yes and instead of praying for what I asked for, they prayed that God would make me sick so that I could stop smoking. I was a babe in Christ back then, but I knew that this was not a prayer that I wanted answered. I stopped them and asked them to leave. They got upset and said I was being disrespectful and spoke ill upon me again.

After they left, I thought about what they prayed over me and why. I mean, what did "sick" look like to them? Was I supposed to throw up every time I smoked a cigarette? Was I supposed to get a sore throat, get cancer or what? Does God answer prayers like that, or does it summon demonic forces to try and manipulate circumstances to fulfill the prayer? Remember sickness is a curse of the law. Jesus redeemed us from the curse of the law at the Cross. Sickness is not God's will, so no God does not answer this type of prayer. Since this type of prayer is not in agreement with God's will, it agrees with the will of the enemy which makes it a soulish prayer.

Despite what the Word of God says, some people believe they've seen answers to these types of prayers. So, if God does not answer these types of prayers, how is it that people believe they've received answers to such prayers? Satan appears as an angel of light to get believers to believe his lies. He can also arrange circumstances, so it looks like the prayer has been answered by God. He tried this with Jesus when He was on the mountain to fast and pray for 40 days (Matthew 4:1-11).

Jesus says we are not to curse others, so how do we curse others? James 3:8-10 tells us:

⁸ But no man can tame the tongue. It is an unruly evil, full of deadly poison. ⁹ With it we bless our God and Father, and with it we curse men, who have been made in the similitude of God. ¹⁰ Out of the same mouth proceed blessing and cursing. My brethren, these things ought not to be so."
— James 3:8-10

This scripture says we can curse others with our mouths. This would be whether in speaking or praying. When a Christian prays in agreement with God's will and His word, we release the power of God into our situation. There are hundreds of promises in the Word of God that we can pray and speak over others. God says that He watches over His word to perform it (Jeremiah 1:12), so if we want our prayer answered we should pray His word.

Angeline L. Williams

Warfare Scriptures

"No weapon that is formed against you will prosper, and every tongue that accuses you in judgment you will condemn. This is the heritage of the servants of the Lord, and their vindication is from Me," declares the Lord." (Isaiah 54:17).

"You are from God, little children, and have overcome them; because greater is He who is in you than he who is in the world." (1 John 4:4)

"For God hath not given us the spirit of fear; but of power, and of love, and of a sound mind. – 2 Timothy 1:7 (KJV)

"No temptation has overtaken you that is not common to man. God is faithful, and he will not let you be tempted beyond your ability, but with the temptation he will also provide the way of escape, that you may be able to endure it." (1 Corinthians 10:13)

"I sought the Lord, and he answered me and delivered me from all my fears." (Psalm 34:4)

"In all these things, we are more than conquerors through

Him who loved us." (Romans 8:37)

"But thanks be to God, who gives us the victory through our Lord Jesus Christ." (1 Corinthians 15:57)

"But the Lord is faithful, and he will strengthen you and protect you from the evil one." (2 Thessalonians 3:3)

"Behold, I have given you authority to tread on serpents and scorpions, and over all the power of the enemy, and nothing shall hurt you." (Luke 10:19)

"The thief comes only to steal and kill and destroy. I came that they may have life and have it abundantly." (John 10:10)

"Truly I tell you, whatever you bind on earth will be bound in heaven, and whatever you loose on earth will be loosed in heaven. Again, truly I tell you that if two of you on earth agree about anything they ask for, it will be done for them by my Father in heaven." (Matthew 18:18-19)

"The Lord will cause your enemies who rise against you to be defeated before you. They shall come out against you one way and flee before you seven ways." (Deuteronomy 28:7)

"I have told you these things, so that in me you may have peace. In this world you will have trouble. But take heart!

I have overcome the world." (John 16:33)

"And you shall know the truth, and the truth shall make you free." (John 8:32)

"And they overcame him by the blood of the Lamb and by the word of their testimony, and they did not love their lives to the death." (Revelation 12:11)

"...On this rock I will build my church, and the gates of hell shall not prevail against it." (Matthew 16:18)

"But those who wait on the Lord shall renew their strength; they shall mount up with wings like eagles, they shall run and not be weary, they shall walk and not faint." (Isaiah 40:31)

"Truly I tell you, if you have faith as small as a mustard seed, you can say to this mountain, 'Move from here to there,' and it will move. Nothing will be impossible for you." (Matthew 17:20)

"You shall not fear them, for it is the Lord your God who fights for you." (Deuteronomy 3:22)

"What then shall we say to these things? If God is for us, who is against us?" (Romans 8:31)

I Don't Believe in Fairytales

"This is what the Lord says to you: 'Do not be afraid or discouraged because of this vast army. For the battle is not yours, but God's." (2 Chronicles 20:15)

Angeline L. Williams

In the Fullness of Time

"God proves to be good to the man who passionately waits, to the woman who diligently seeks. It's a good thing to quietly hope, quietly hope for help from God. It's a good thing when you're young to stick it out through the hard times. When life is heavy and hard to take, go off by yourself. Enter the silence. Bow in prayer. Don't ask questions: Wait for hope to appear." —Lamentations 3:25-29, The Message).

There are some Christians who don't struggle with not being in a romantic relationship or seemingly sexual temptation. They are content. I'm not one of those people. God made Eve for Adam, and He made me for somebody, know what I mean? In fact, most single Christians would rather be married. God is a keeper. He has kept me for many years, but for someone who desires to be married, there are times when being single can be difficult.

As a single Christian, there have been times when I felt out of place at family gatherings, social groups, church, and other events. There have been times when I have expressed discontent with being single and my desire to be married to fellow believers, and I walked away feeling as if my desire was somehow dishonoring God. As if wanting to be married and loving God with all my heart are at odds.

Married people have said I don't know how blessed I am to be single because I have more time for the things of God. You've probably heard something similar. You may have even felt guilty for being unhappy about being single. The Bible does not condemn the desire to be married. God designed marriage before the fall, so the desire to be married is normal.

There is nothing wrong with being single or not wanting to be single either. Being discontent with being single is not a sign that you are discontent with God. However, if your whole life seems to revolve around finding a mate and hinders your joy in God, then you have a problem.

After the decision to follow Christ or not, the next major decision we will ever make is who we marry. Do not be so anxious that you miss the red flags. Red flags are God's way of saying stop.

Different beliefs of faith (not levels) is a huge red flag. The Apostle Paul warned us not to marry someone who doesn't share our beliefs and spiritual commitments.

> *"14 Do not be unequally yoked together with unbelievers. For what fellowship has righteousness with lawlessness? And what communion has light with darkness? 15 And what accord has Christ with Belial? Or what part has a believer with an unbeliever?"* —2 Corinthians 6:14-15

For instance, Proverbs 22:24 says, *"Make no friendship with an angry man, and with a furious man do not go."* A relationship with an angry person can be bad, and it can also be a warning to someone contemplating marriage that an abusive marriage is on the horizon. Laziness is another warning sign we should not ignore as we get to know potential marriage partners.

Like many Christians, I am still working on becoming more patient. When God? How long God? What am I missing God? I have often cried, but God does not move on our timing for anything. In the process of God moving me closer to patience, I've learned that He is always right on time for whatever I need Him to do.

As I look back over my life, I marvel at how often something I prayed for, yearned for, waited for, and cried for finally came to fruition just in time. If you're honest, you can probably see that God's provision, protection, mercy, and love have always occurred just in the nick of time in your life as well. Just as God has been on time for everything else my spouse will come at just the right time. If I never get married, I am okay with that too. I'm learning not to take matters into my own hands and let God do His thing.

I've also learned that God desires the kind of close interaction with us as that of a spouse. He's an up-close, hands-on, how-was-your-day, cares about even the smallest details of your life kind of God. I've learned that this closeness with God is what I want above anything else. This did not happen overnight. It took some time for me to grasp that I had to let Him be this kind of God and include Him in everything.

When it comes to God connecting you and your mate, only He knows when that will be. We cannot rush or alter God's plan to prosper you. "In the fullness of time," God will present you to each other. In the meantime, you can begin to pray for your spouse and your life together now.

Although God takes us through a make-ready process this doesn't mean that you or your mate must be perfect before God brings you together. From my experience, God continues to work on us every day, married or single. So, if you are waiting for perfection in you, or a potential mate you will probably never get married. But I do believe if you allow God to make you ready for marriage it will help your marriage in the long run. In the meantime, you can also begin to pray for your spouse and your life together now.

The word tells us to pray about everything and for everyone. Praying for your future spouse should be included. Regarding the husband dream God said, "*Husband, pray.*" I believe that was a clear instruction to pray for my future husband. I want to encourage you to pray for your future spouse, rather than just praying for God to send them!

What should prayer for a future spouse look like? What do I pray for the guy in the dream? I pray for his relationship with the Lord. That he would surrender all to God through Jesus Christ.

Since husbands are called to wash their wives with the water of the Word of God, I prayed that he will have a desire to consistently study God's word (Ephesians 5:25-26).

I pray the scriptures that I continually pray for everyone in Ephesians 1:17-21 and Ephesians 3:15-19. God may lead you to pray for other things. If God says pray about it or for it, then do it.

I don't know all there is to know about prayer, but I do know that God hears our prayers when we pray according to His word. I don't know if your prayers will lead you to your mate, but I do know that when we pray for someone else, it changes us in the process. I also know that not one prayer prayed is wasted.

There is so much more that I would love to share that will you walk in the victory of Christ that it would take several books, so I invite you to follow me on my blog at: www.angelinelwilliams.com.

About the Author

Prophetess Angeline L. Williams is a submitted vessel of God who flows in the ministry gifts of prophet, evangelist, pastor, and teacher. God has led her to influence many individuals into a restored relationship with Jesus Christ. Her passion for God and His Word has led to an anointing to preach and teach the Word of God with authority, revelation, and deliverance. In 2002, she received her license and ordination to preach the gospel, assuming the roles of prophet, evangelist, pastor, and teacher.

Her books and messages are illuminated with revelation, personal testimony, and a depth of wisdom, and insight resulting from decades of study, and relationship with God. She is the owner of Williams DocuPrep, where she has been providing self-publishing services to authors, and independent publishers since 2005. Visit her website at www.williamsdocuprep.com to learn more.

I Don't Believe in Fairytales

"The Spirit of the Lord is upon me, because he hath anointed me to preach the gospel to the poor; he hath sent me to heal the brokenhearted, to preach deliverance to the captives, and recovering of sight to the blind, to set at liberty them that are bruised, to preach the acceptable year of the Lord." — Luke 4:18-19

Meet Jesus

Want to become a child of God? Do you recognize that you are a sinner? Do you believe in what Christ has done? As a sign of turning from sin, we begin by asking Jesus to come into our heart. This is also called the 'Salvation Prayer' or the 'Sinners prayer'.

The Bible says in 1 John 1:9 *"If we confess our sins, he is faithful and just to forgive us our sins and to cleanse us from all unrighteousness."* You can do this anytime and anywhere. (You are then putting your life into God's control and saying that from that moment you will follow and serve Jesus alone.) So you can literally pray something out of your mouth like this:

Lord Jesus, I know that I am a sinner. The sinful life that I lived separated me from you. I ask You to forgive me of my sins. I believe that you died on the cross and rose on the third day to pay my sin debt. Lord, I'm sorry for my sins. From this day forward, I want to put all my trust in you, Lord show me how to live a Christian life. In Jesus name, Amen.

If you have prayed this prayer from the bottom of your heart, you now have Jesus in your heart. Now tell someone what you have done! Spread the good news.

P.S. ... I would love to rejoice with you in your decision to follow Christ. Let me know by completing the form at my website: www.angelinelwilliams.com/contact.html

Other Books by Angeline

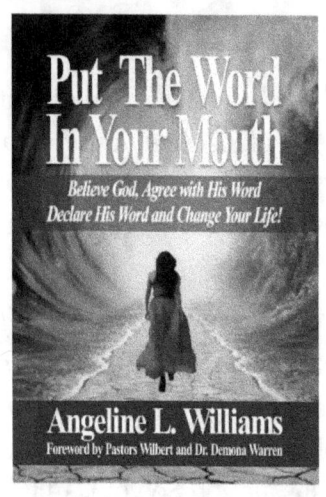

www.ingramcontent.com/pod-product-compliance
Lightning Source LLC
Chambersburg PA
CBHW071209070526
44584CB00019B/2975